# Hand-Feeding Wild Birds

*Written by: Hugh Wiberg*

**First Edition**

Annedawn Publishing
Partners
P.O. Box 247, Norton, MA 02766

# Hand Feeding Wild Birds

*Written by: Hugh Wiberg*

Annedawn Publishing
Partners
P.O. Box 247–B, Norton,MA 02766

Copyright 1993 by Hugh Wiberg
First Printing 1993
Printed in the United States of America
Library of Congress Cataloging in Publication Data
Wiberg, Hugh
Hand-Feeding Wild Birds / by Hugh Wiberg
1st edition.
Library of Congress Catalog Card Number 93-071940

ISBN 0-9632793-2-7

All photos in this book were taken by the author, unless otherwise noted.

There exists for all of us a need
to find ways to set aside, for a time, the
stress and trials of everyday life.

*Hugh Wiberg*

This book is dedicated to the
loving memory of my mother,
Mary Wiberg, who is now
feeding birds in a
Better Place.

# Table of Contents

*Right Page: A White-breasted Nuthatch inspects the menu just before coming to the hand.*

## About the Author

Hugh Wiberg was born in Newark, New Jersey of minister parents, the third of eight children. He received his education at Trinity College, Hartford, Connecticut and Northeastern University, Boston, Massachusetts. Hugh worked for many years for the Carters' Ink Company of Cambridge, MA, and later for the Dennison Manufacturing Co., of Framingham, MA in various sales and marketing capacities.

In 1972, Mr. Wiberg wrote **Backyard Vegetable Gardening for the Beginner** which went to three editions. Currently Hugh is a manager at Mahoney's Rocky Ledge Nursery in Winchester, MA. His spare time activities include writing a gardening column, "guesting" on a Boston radio talk show fielding questions on the subjects of gardening and birds, and "birding", whenever his busy schedule allows.

Another of Wiberg's hobbies is growing giant pumpkins. Hugh, with his pumpkin-growing partner Tom Cone, of Andover, MA, placed second at the 1992 Topsfield Fair's All New England Pumpkin Weigh-Off with a 582-pound Dill's Atlantic Giant Pumpkin!

Wiberg lives with his lovely wife Barbara in Wilmington, MA, and looks forward to spending three weeks each year, in early February, searching for unusual birds in the Florida Everglades.

Hugh's granddaughter Alexis appears in this book at one and two years of age, with chickadees on her hand, proving it is never too early to begin learning *Hand-Feeding Wild Birds*.

*Below: The author patiently coaxes this black-cap as their eyes meet in admiration of one another. Photo by Mike Pigeon of the Lowell Sun.*

## Acknowledgements

I would like to thank the following people, who encouraged and assisted me during the writing and publishing of this book:

John V. Dennis, Dr. Roger Tory Peterson, Donald Hyde, Michael Corral, Meg Courtney, Editorial Assistant, Robert Ives, Thomas W. Lyle and most notably, Donald Langevin, Publisher, Annedawn Publishing.

A special acknowledgement is necessary for a person in whom I placed much responsibility, yet shares none of the attention which may result from the publishing of this book. My wife, Barbara Wiberg, labored many hours, typing, editing and proofreading my work. Her contributions can never be really understood by anyone other than myself. Without her, this book would never have been published.

*Hugh Wiberg*

*Right: The author ponders which woodland path to take, before setting-out on a crisp, November morning with a pocket full of sunflower seeds.*

## Foreword

During spare moments in his busy life, Hugh Wiberg has centered his attention upon a single facet of bird feeding. His goal has been to hand-feed some of the birds that come to his feeders or that he encounters on his walks. He has been doing this for about 15 years at his home and in woodlands in eastern Massachusetts. Having achieved success with a number of species, he next turned his talents to taking photographs of birds on the hand. His success in this area can be seen in the excellent color photographs on the pages that follow. Finally, he has ably captured the excitement and rewards of hand-feeding in the written word.

What has impressed me most about this undertaking is that Wiberg has chosen a subject that some regard as already adequately treated. Living as he does in New England, he is in a region where bird-feeding had its early roots. Almost a hundred years ago, pioneers in bird-feeding were coaxing birds to their hands and even lips. One has only to read *Wild Bird Guests* by Ernest Harold Baynes, published in 1915. This was followed by *Hand-Taming Wild Birds* at the Feeder by Alfred G. Martin. Martin's book, published in 1967, contained what many, including myself, regarded as the last word on hand-taming. I had the privilege of visiting the author at this home near Bangor, Maine. Here, living a Thoreau-like existence, Martin conducted his taming experiments. I was very much impressed by his dedication to this pursuit and his love for animals of all kinds.

Alfred Martin had an advantage not enjoyed by Hugh Wiberg. Many of the birds coming to his feeders over the years were already partly tame. Far northern birds, such as the Gray Jay, Common Redpoll, Pine Grosbeak, and Evening Grosbeak, have little fear of man. They can readily be induced to feed from the hand. But these invaders from the north have not been coming as far south in recent years. Warmer winters and more plentiful food in the North seem to be the reasons. Thus Hugh Wiberg in Massachusetts has missed out on some of the most receptive birds of all.

But like Martin, he has the ubiquitous Black-capped Chickadee to work with. As I know from experience in the wilds of New England, an occasional Black-cap will come to your hand for food without any previous overtures on your part. Hugh, unlike Martin, also has the Northern Cardinal and Tufted Titmouse in his yard. These two, along with the Red-Bellied Woodpecker, Mockingbird, and Carolina Wren, are southern birds that have pushed into New England since the days of John James Audubon. Again, warmer winters and adequate food supplies have brought them north.

It is not Hugh's purpose to see how many kinds of birds he can hand-feed. For him, encouraging birds to take food from the hand is not a game or sport like bird listing. Rather it is a way to become better acquainted with birds. Devoid of their inherent fear of man, birds are much more likely to reveal their true selves.

This was something that was discovered by Len Howard, the British bird behaviorist, whose writings inspired interest around the middle of this century.

One may ask how Hugh's methods differ from those of others. Unlike either Martin or Miss Howard, he does not talk to the birds he is hand-feeding, nor does he think it important to refrain from swallowing. Forsaking the comforts of home, he sallies forth on cold winter days to visit woodlands and nature preserves. Here he begins his routine of offering birds food at selected sites. First he watches at a distance and then over a period of weeks approaches more closely with food in his outstretched hand. Through patience, perseverance, and avoidance of sudden movement, he gradually wins over once wary birds.

Hugh assures his readers that hand-feeding in no way makes a bird dependent upon us or poses a danger to it. Nevertheless, I should point out that hand-fed birds in one's yard can make a nuisance of themselves by following us when we are outside and by tapping upon windows. Hand-feeding is not something to be undertaken lightly. Read what Hugh has to say about it and then make up your mind.

John V. Dennis

Nantucket, Massachusetts

Princess Anne, Maryland

*Right: John V. and Mary Alice Dennis vacationing in Switzerland in October, 1991.*

**Publisher's Note**

John V. Dennis is a renowned writer of books related to birds and "birding". He has written numerous books and hundreds of articles on the subject, and his name is a household word among avid bird watchers. To his credit, Mr. Dennis has written such well-known titles as, **"A Complete Guide to Bird Feeding"**, 1975, **"Beyond the Bird Feeder"**, 1981, **"The Wildlife Gardener"**, 1985, **"The Great Cypress Swamps"**, 1988 and **"A Guide to Western Bird Feeding"**, 1991.

## Introduction

In our increasingly complex lives there seems never to be enough time to stand back and enjoy the world around us. The closest some of us come to experiencing the wonders of nature is through watching the National Geographic programs and the Nature series on public television. Those of us fortunate enough to live in suburban or rural areas may also set up a bird feeder or two in our backyards. At last count, more than 65,000,000 Americans are feeding wild birds. Several million people belong to bird clubs and associations.

Wild birds are among the earth's most beautiful creatures. Confirmed "birders" take great pleasure studying our avian neighbors at a distance, ranging from ten to fifteen feet at our feeders to a quarter of a mile or more through spotting scopes and binoculars.

*Left: The author, Hugh Wiberg introduces his one-year-old granddaughter, Alexis, to the curiosity and joy of hand-feeding wild birds. Photo by Wendy Wiberg, the author's daughter. Above: The odds against photographing two different species on the hand at the same time are enormous. The author is quick to concede that there was more luck than skill involved in "shooting" this chickadee and nuthatch.*

Many years ago, partly by accident, partly by design, I discovered that many of our resident birds will tolerate the close presence of their human neighbors in exchange for a free meal. This was no major break-through, certainly, for many others besides this author have experienced the special thrill of having a wild bird perch on the hand. Roger Tory Peterson tells me that he has brought several species of birds to his hand over his illustrious 80-plus years. I suspect that our North American Indians were hand-feeding Black-capped Chickadees long before Columbus set sail for the New World.

There exists for all of us a need to find ways to set aside for a time the stress and trials of everyday life. Some choose gardening, others exercise, or read, or make stained-glass ornaments, or watch television. I have found that the very best short-term "escape" for me is taking a walk in a wildlife sanctuary with a pocket full of sunflower seeds. Nothing relaxes me more than the fresh air, the moderate exercise, and the wonder of what may be waiting for me around the next bend in the path.

My introduction to hand-feeding wild birds originated in an Audubon sanctuary north of Boston. I recount those early experiences in Chapter 4 on chickadees. Since then I have hand-fed birds in my own backyard in Wilmington, Massachusetts, at several other Massachusetts sanctuaries, and as far afield as Sarasota, Florida. This pastime has given me so much pleasure over the years that I have decided it is time to share the fun.

Of course everyone who reads this book will not be motivated to try his or her luck at hand-feeding birds. A small percentage of readers will want to experiment with this aspect of birding, and for that reason I have attempted to provide some simple guidelines which have consistently

worked for me. I believe that less than half of those who will try hand-feeding wild birds will succeed. This is because most people do not have the patience required to gain the confidence of their winged subjects. To be successful, this activity requires repeated attempts, following my pro-

cedures, to bring a wild bird to the hand. The only exception would be accidentally crossing paths with birds (probably Black-capped Chickadees) which have already learned to take seeds from humans.

I would stress here that it is not our goal or desire to "tame" wild birds through hand-feeding. What happens is that we are modifying the bird's behavior similar to setting up a bird feeder in our backyard. In Chapter 10 we will consider the question of "intrusiveness."

Think of hand-feeding birds as a process, not as an event. To succeed you will have to summon all of your reserves of patience and persever-

*Left Page*
*Top: The author landed several Scrub Jays while vacationing in Florida. This individual had been banded in an effort to protect and restore this once very common cousin of the northern Blue Jay.*
*Bottom: A Scrub Jay in Florida is obviously not quite clear on the concept of hand-feeding.*
*Right Page: Two chickadees proudly pose for a rare group photo.*

ance. If you do not succeed, you will at the very least enjoy all of the physical and psychological rewards of taking a walk in the woods.

This book is intended to help bring bird lovers into close and personal touch with our native wild birds.

*Below: This titmouse, early in our acquaintance, preferred to stand on a large rock at first, but was soon flying directly to the hand for food.*

## Chapter One—Birds that will Hand-Feed and where to find them

Of the estimated 65,000,000 people in North America who put out feed for wild birds, the number of folks who have had a bird come to the hand is extremely small. This is because there is a general consensus among those of us who feed the birds that nature has "programmed" these feathered creatures to avoid, at all cost, very close proximity with humans.

When we restock our backyard feeders, the birds in the area scatter immediately. You may have noticed, though, that Black-capped Chickadees are the last to depart as you approach the feeder. From time to time we will see, in the newspaper or on a bag of sunflower seed, a photo of a chickadee perched on a human hand. Whenever the subject of hand-feeding comes up, we automatically think of chickadees.

*Below: After landing on a human hand, chickadees sometimes pause for a second or two before selecting a seed, as if to check-out their benefactor.*

I have enjoyed my very personal experiences with Black-caps enough that I was motivated to experiment with other winter resident birds here in the northeast. Some of those efforts succeeded; others failed entirely. The birds I have brought to my hand, at our backyard feeders in Wilmington, Massachusetts and at several woodland locations in our home state are:

Black-capped Chickadees

Tufted Titmice

Red-breasted Nuthatches

White-breasted Nuthatches

Downy Woodpeckers

*Above: A January morning in a Massachusetts wildlife sanctuary. Below: A "red-breast" searches for the best morsel before flying to a nearby tree where it will be hidden for future consumption.*

In addition, I have had the following birds as close to my hand as 12 to 18 inches, which encourages me that if I were to take the additional time required, I can probably "land":

White-throated Sparrows

Mockingbirds

Purple Finches

House Finches

I have also hand-fed Scrub Jays and female Boat-tailed Grackles while on vacation in Florida (see Chapter 8). There has been little formal research done on the subject of hand-feeding birds. One of the major limiting factors in research is the time required to condition a single bird (the exception being chickadees) to take food from the hand.

My time-limited efforts to hand-feed wild birds leads me to believe that, with persistence, some individual birds from most species of the eastern woodland can be encouraged to hand-feed. I say "some individuals" because, even with Black-caps, there will always be a percentage of birds in every species which will never take food from a human.

*Below: A titmouse looks over the rations before selecting a nut meat and quickly departing.*

I have not set out to compile a long list of species that have, or will eventually, come to my hand. My hand-feeding activities are limited by work and family obligations, and I doubt that I will ever succeed in bringing more than a dozen different birds to my hand. I have set aside some leisure time to this hobby because I enjoy combining my exercise regimen with hand-feeding, and I experience much pleasure in making personal (and not harmfully intrusive) contact with wild creatures. Except on special occasions, my hand-feeding activities rarely consume more than two or three hours a week from late October through March.

In the early '60s, Alfred G. Martin, a Maine outdoorsman, wrote *Hand-Taming Wild Birds at the Feeder*. Martin experimented with some of the common woodland birds of central Maine and hand-fed the following birds:

> Pine and Evening Grosbeaks
>
> Purple Finches
>
> Redpolls
>
> Cedar Waxwings
>
> Catbirds
>
> Ruby-throated Hummingbirds
>
> Chickadees

He attempted to hand-feed both Red-and White-breasted Nuthatches, without success. His efforts were not limited to exclusively winter hand-feeding.

I might add parenthetically that I have noticed a disturbing trend over the last 30 years relative to the declining number of species of wild birds frequenting our woodlands and backyard feeders. As an example, my notes from the winters 1968 to 1970 reveal that we viewed an average of 24 species of birds each winter at our Wilmington, Massachusetts feeders. By contrast, the last three years, 1991-1993, we are averaging just 15 species. Notable by their absence in recent years are Redpolls, Pine Siskins, Grosbeaks, American Tree Sparrows, and Fox Sparrows, among others.

Undoubtedly one very important reason for this decline is the diminution of wildlife habitat here in eastern Massachusetts. In addition, there are the addition factors of environmental changes and short- and long-term climatological changes.

The message appears to be, enjoy what we have while we have it; the trend is not encouraging.

Newcomers to hand-feeding will want to begin experimenting with Black-capped Chickadees. They are by far the easiest species to bring to the hand.

From my experience, here is a list in descending order of the "easiest", to "hardest" hand-feeders.

1. Black-capped Chickadees
2. Tufted Titmice
3. Red-breasted Nuthatches
4. White-breasted Nuthatches
5. Downy Woodpeckers
6. White-throated Sparrows
7. Mockingbirds
8. Cardinals

My tentative efforts to bring Blue Jays, Crows and Mourning Doves to my hand have been unsuccessful so far.

In Florida, watch for Scrub Jays and Boat-tailed Grackles (especially females), two species which seem very willing to take food from human hands.

The best places to find the birds mentioned in this book are in the remaining relatively undisturbed woodlands of your state. Wildlife sanctuar-

*Below: A very aggressive Red-breasted Nuthatch quickly disperses a pair of chickadees in its quest of a quick morsel.*

ies are excellent because they tend to be protected from wholesale human intrusion. And, of course, our backyard bird-feeders, even with declining bird populations, are a constant source of hand-feeding opportunities.

*Above: Two Black-capped Chickadees arrive at the hand at the same time. The chickadee on the left, the more dominant of the two, succeeds in ushering the other chickadee away.*
*Right Page: The common crow will rarely allow humans to get closer than 35 or 40 feet. These three (one in the tree) would fly off whenever the author attempted to approach closer.*

*Above: At a secluded bridge in a Massachusetts wildlife sanctuary, three chickadees inspect a freshly set table.*

# Chapter Two—Time of the Year, Weather Conditions, Best Foods

Except for a dozen or so Black-capped Chickadees who live in my neighborhood and take sunflower seeds from my hand the year round, my activities with hand-feeding are confined to the five months from November through March. There are several reasons for this, including:

## Survival Time

Winter is survival time for the birds. Our severe New England winters put great stress on all of the animals and birds to simply survive. Without insects, the native wild birds must constantly scramble to find enough residual bits of fruit, vegetable matter, seeds, and berries to carry them through until spring. Most birds, the exceptions being the very young, the very old and the injured or diseased, manage quite well in spite of occasional sub-zero temperatures.

Backyard bird feeders give the birds a tremendous boost over the winter months. It is important that our feeders are kept consistently stocked starting in November, since some birds will become partially dependent on them until late in March.

Because food is scarce in the winter, the birds are more inclined to risk closer contact with humans in exchange for food. In my experience with hand-feeding, the chickadees, nuthatches, and titmice are far more willing to learn to hand-feed in January than they are in July.

## Summer is Rearing -Time for Wild Birds

The wild birds are rearing their young during the warmer months. Along with there being a bountiful supply of natural foods available from spring through fall, the parent birds' time is devoted almost entirely to caring for this year's brood, and, in some cases, broods. With the constant busyness of feeding and protecting their young, the older birds do not have time in the spring and summer to learn to know and trust a human offering handouts.

## Summer is Busy-Time for Human Beings

Busy summer schedules do not allow sufficient time for hand-feeding. Again, success with hand-feeding birds is not a one- or two-shot process. Most of us are so occupied during the spring and summer months with gardens, cookouts, lawn mowing, and vacations that visiting a sanctuary or nearby woodland on several consecutive weekends to hand-feed birds is out of the question. We are simply too busy at this "outdoors" time of year to seriously pursue this activity. When November arrives, our weekends become much less hectic and, if we choose to, we can begin to think about coaxing a chickadee out of a shrub and onto our hand. In Chapter 3 we will learn how to do exactly that.

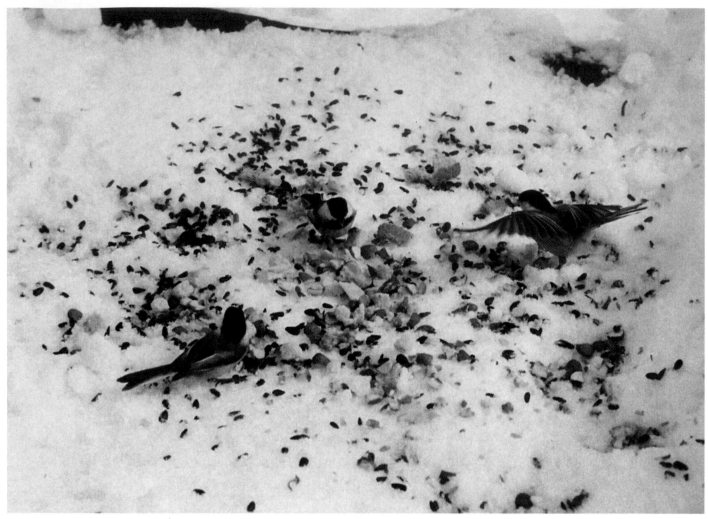

*Above: The chickadees are usually the first birds to arrive, soon after the day's fare is scattered on the snow.*

## WEATHER CONDITIONS

Depending on many weather-related factors, the probability of succeeding with hand-feeding can fluctuate wildly. Several years ago someone asked me to describe the absolute optimum time and weather conditions for successful hand-feeding. My answer was that all of the following would be present:

- ✔ A day in February
- ✔ 7:00 to 9:30 A.M.
- ✔ 24 hours after a severe ice storm
- ✔ bright sunshine
- ✔ outdoor temperature from 10 to 15 degrees Fahrenheit
- ✔ little or no wind

Although all of the five months from November through March have excellent potential for hand-feeding wild birds, I have had best results in February. I am sure this is because February is the last bitterly cold month here in New England, and the surviving birds are more physically stressed during this month than at any time of the year. This being the case, it is not too surprising that in February the resident chickadees, titmice, and nuthatches, among others, are most ready and willing to take food whenever and wherever it is offered, including directly from a human hand.

As to the time of day, from sunrise to 9:30 A.M. is the busiest part of day for the birds. You may have noticed that there is usually much activity around your feeder first thing in the morning. After ten hours of fasting overnight, it is necessary for the birds to locate food quickly after daybreak in order to refuel their engines. I have had my very best hand-feeding experiences between the hours of 7:00 and 9:30 A.M.

## Ice

Here in the northeast, we will experience an intense ice storm perhaps one winter out of three. In spite of the almost magical beauty such an event produces, I hate to see the trees and branches covered with ice because I know the birds are going to suffer as a result. A sheet of ice on the trees effectively takes away a large part of the birds' winter food, in the form of insects in several stages of dormant metamorphosis. Fortunately an ice coating usually melts within 24 to 48 hours, but in the meantime it can be touch-and-go for the birds. I recall that the very busiest hand-feeding occasions I have had, what can be referred to as "feeding frenzies," took place within a day or two of an ice storm.

## Cold

Although most of us (myself included) will probably not spend a great deal of time attempting to hand-feed birds when the temperature is hovering between 10 to 20 degrees above zero, severe cold weather will noticeably increase your odds for success. The birds' heart rates are increased then to provide additional life sustaining heat, and a steady supply of food becomes critical. Here again you will note increased activity at your feeder when the temperature drops sharply, and the chickadees seem most willing at these times to take food from the hand.

## Wind

I mention "little or no wind" only because you and I are not going to be willing to spend more than a few minutes attempting to hand-feed when the wind chill factor is around 20 degrees below zero. Choose a day to experiment when there is little or no wind in the forecast.

For the above reasons, your hand-feeding experiments, in order to have the best chance for success, are best concentrated in the five months from November through March.

## BEST FOODS

I have experimented the last several winters with different foods. The objective of these experiments was to see which foods are most desired by chickadees, titmice, and both of our common nuthatches.

When I began hand-feeding wild birds, I used exclusively sunflower seed, both oil and striped, because I knew that most of our common winter birds consume this seed at our feeders. In the ensuing winters I have tried the so called "mixed" seed, hulled (shell-less) sunflower seed and various nut meats, including walnut, filbert, almond, pecan, and Brazil. Based on these trials, I would list the order of preference as follows, from most to least desirable:

| RANK | FOOD | DESIRABILITY RATING |
|------|------|---------------------|
| 1 | filbert | 10 |
| 2 | pecan | 9.5 |
| 3 | walnut | 9.5 |
| 4 | Brazil | 9 |
| 5 | hulled sunflower | 8.5 |
| 6 | almond | 8 |
| 7 | oil sunflower | 7 |
| 8 | striped sunflower | 5 |
| 9 | mixed seed | 3 |

Don't waste your time with mixed seed; the birds will pick out the few sunflower seeds and ignore the rest.

The nut meats should be broken into bits about the size of a pea.

My suggestion for beginners is that you start with hulled sunflower seeds, high on the birds' "desirable" list, and considerably less expensive than nut meats.

Below: A White-breasted Nuthatch holds a piece of nut meat
while inquizzitively eyeing the host.

Above: During the "getting to know you period" this
Red-breasted Nuthatch allowed the author to approach within
two feet before darting off.

# Chapter 3—How To Hand-Feed Wild Birds

In this chapter, I shall describe the simple procedures which have brought wild birds to my hand.

I suspect that most "birders" who will decide to experiment with hand-feeding will begin in their own backyards, for the simple reasons of convenience and accessibility. My guess is that many readers already have feeders in their yards, and are quite familiar with the eight or ten species which we consider "regular" visitors. Let's start in the backyard and then proceed to a rather different approach to hand-feeding in woodlands and wildlife sanctuaries.

## HAND-FEEDING AT THE BACKYARD FEEDER

If you have had one or more bird feeders in your yard for at least a year, you already have a head start toward hand-feeding. Chances are you have a small contingent of Black-capped Chickadees who show up to take advantage of your hospitality every day. Assuming your feeder is typical, titmice, nuthatches, and several species of finches along with an occasional woodpecker, are also in evidence most days. If you scatter a little mixed seed on the ground, you will have sparrows, Mourning Doves, juncos, and Cardinals. (And yes, probably squirrels!)

If you do not have a feeder in the yard, your first step will be to set one up in the fall or early winter. Unless you are in a very urban setting, you will soon have birds showing up for free meals. Once you have a regular clientele you can begin to experiment. Starting out you should think in terms of bringing a chickadee to hand, since this species is by far the easiest to hand-feed. Here is how I have brought Black-capped Chickadees to my hand in my backyard.

The feeder I chose to work with happened to be the wooden "covered-bridge" style, atop a six-foot pole protected by a squirrel baffle. Beginning early in November on Saturday and Sunday mornings, I went out and stood near a maple tree which was about 15 feet from the feeder. I remained as motionless as possible, and in a few minutes the birds began to appear. First the chickadees, than the finches (gold, house and purple) then a titmouse or two, and soon a White-breasted Nuthatch. As long as I remained still, they came and went almost as though I was not there. The first three weekends I simply repeated this process, making no move toward the feeder.

On the fourth Saturday, I moved five paces toward the feeder and turned into a statue. In less than a minute, several chickadees were at the feeder, seemingly oblivious to my presence. It took a few minutes longer for the other species to appear, but eventually all of the "regulars" were flying back and forth to the feeder.

My visits to the feeder lasted between 20 and 30 minutes on those Saturday and Sunday mornings, after which I slowly walked back to the

*Below: A hand-feeder near Sarasota, Florida brings a Scrub Jay onto his hand for a sunflower seed.*

house. On each succeeding Saturday morning, I closed the gap by a foot or two. By the sixth weekend I was standing only four feet away. With little hesitation, after the passage of no more than a minute or two, the Black-caps would appear and commence to feed. I noticed that the other species stopped coming to the feeder once I was closer than five feet.

Gradually the chickadees had become conditioned to accepting my close proximity, since I remained quite motionless and posed them no threat. As soon as I would back up to eight or ten feet, the titmice and nuthatches, keeping a close eye on me, would begin to feed again.

*Left: Summoning lots of patience, this first-time visitor to a Massachusetts wildlife sanctuary was able to "land" a chickadee in 15 minutes. Photo by Wendy Wiberg.*

Although I chose to remain standing during my weekend visits to this feeder, you may find it more comfortable to sit nearby on a chair or a stepladder. However you make your approach, the keys here are silence and an absolute absence of motion.

Finally, on the eighth weekend I went on to the next step. That Friday night, I set up a six-foot step ladder close to the feeder. The next morning I emptied the feeder and sat on the step ladder so that I could place my hand into the feeder. At the far end I placed a dozen sunflower seeds and, at the end closest to me, I rested my hand holding several seeds. In a few minutes, I saw several chickadees looking at me from a nearby lilac shrub. Soon a single Black-cap flew over, landed at the opposite end, snatched a seed and darted away. Quickly the other chickadees moved in and the dozen seeds soon disappeared. Now the only seeds in the feeder were on my hand. Success did not happen immediately. A chickadee landed near my hand, stared at me for a moment, and flew off. I began to wonder if this was as close as I would get. Two or three other chickadees flew onto the feeder, also checked me over, and also flew away. I decided to leave it there for that weekend.

*Below: Two chickadees eye each other in the frantic coming-and-going of hand feeding.*

This was now becoming a regular half-hour Saturday and Sunday morning ritual. I was enjoying it becuse it wasn't taking more time than I could afford, and I seemed to be making good progress.

On the succeeding two weekends, I repeated this last process with the same results. The weekend after that (the eleventh Saturday and Sunday overall) I "landed" the first blackcap. On this weekend I did not place the dozen seeds at the far end of the feeder. I rested my hand containing several seeds in the middle of the tray and waited. Soon two chickadees landed at the same moment, several inches from my hand. The dominant

*Above: If there are chickadees in the area, they will quickly discover a free meal scatterd on the snow on a cold winter day.*

Black-cap immediately flared his (or her) wings and hissed the second bird away. A moment later the remaining bird was standing on my index finger. I must admit to feeling a quick adrenaline charge, as he/she selected a seed, looked at me for a split second, and was gone. In a minute or two another chickadee, perhaps the same one, landed directly on my hand, took a seed, and flew off. I stayed another ten minutes, as this individual was now coming to my hand with no further hesitation.

The following Friday evening, I removed the feeder entirely. The next morning I sat on the ladder with seeds on my hand. The resident flock of chickadees numbered about a dozen, and on that first "feederless" Saturday morning three or four individuals quickly came to my hand. After 20 minutes of hand-feeding, I replaced the feeder in order to accommodate the other birds in the neighborhood, and went back to the house.

Before the winter was over, almost all of the resident chickadees were hand-feeding. I suspect that several of them eventually came to my hand after seeing their mates doing so over and over. Once the natural barrier was broken through, these Black-caps, when they happened to be in the neighborhood, would invariably fly over to a bush close to me the year around. As often as not, since I usually carry a few sunflower seeds in a pocket, their unspoken requests for a snack would be rewarded.

*Below: A dominant member of the group aggressively asserts his authority, while the others cower and obey.*

Although 99 percent of chickadees are clones of each other and are therefore indistinguishable one from another, I believe that once a Black-cap begins to hand-feed, it will continue to do so for the rest of its life. Because of their similarity, it is next to impossible to keep track of individuals.

You will read in the next chapter about five chickadees I was able to keep track of due to unusual physical markings or deformities.

## HAND-FEEDING IN THE WOODS OR SANCTUARIES

One of my very favorite recreational activities is taking a walk in a wildlife sanctuary or state park. This activity allows me to combine the benefits which come from walking with studying and enjoying the resident wildlife. With a little patience and perseverance, the visitor to a sanctuary or woodland can come to know the resident birds in a very close and intimate way. From notes I took at the time, here is how I brought birds to my hand in a woodland not previously frequented by hand feeders.

Dressed warmly to ward off the 20 F. weather, I set out early on a crisp December morning, bound for a nearby state park. I had with me a small bag which contained hulled sunflower seeds, cheese crackers, and bread scraps. About a mile into the woods, I came across a fallen pine tree which afforded me a comfortable place on which to sit. In a small clearing 20 feet from the fallen tree, I scattered the contents of the food bag onto an area four-feet across. Then I returned to the log and waited.

Having taken walks in this state park on several occasions, I knew there were usually chickadees and nuthatches in this general vicinity. Sure enough, in less than five minutes a pair of chickadees appeared, and flew

*Below: Two chickadees appear to be undecided as to who's turn it is at hand-feeding.*

directly down to the dinner table. Soon three or four more Black-caps appeared, and then a White-breasted Nuthatch flew over to see what was happening. I remained stock still, and I was not sure that the birds knew I was sitting close by. The nuthatch was quickly busying himself with stashing bits of food behind loose bark on nearby trees. I sat and watched, and after 20 minutes I took a head count. My best guess was that there were eight or ten chickadees flitting back and forth, along with a solitary titmouse and one nuthatch. Two White-throated Sparrows had heard the little commotion, and were running back and forth from under a nearby shrub, helping themselves to bits of bread and crackers. By remaining motionless, I might as well not have been there at all.

I returned to this spot the next morning, a Sunday, and repeated the process. On this second day three titmice joined in, along with what were probably the same eight or ten chickadees. The nuthatch was not around, but several Blue jays came by to watch. They spotted me and would not approach closer than 40 feet. After three-quarters of an hour, I left the area and finished my walk.

On the five following weekends, I spent an hour on Saturday and Sunday mornings at this same spot. Since the state park is only eight miles from home, the time involved was not an inconvenience. I carried with me a small collapsible stool, since I was gradually decreasing the distance between me and the food. The stool was more comfortable than sitting on the frozen ground. By the fifth weekend I was sitting six feet from the birds' "dinner table." Predictably on each visit, the chickadees would come in first, usually within 10 minutes of my arrival. Sometimes two or three titmice would appear, along with a White-breasted Nuthatch and, very rarely, a Red-breasted Nuthatch. By now, having become acclimated to my non-threatening presence, the Black-caps were flying directly to the food as soon as they appeared. I noticed that the only times the birds were aware of my presence was when I coughed or shifted my weight. It was evident that the first and most important rule in hand feeding was — and still is — imitate a statue, and, in 15 minutes or less it will be as though you have disappeared.

*Below: Before a White-breasted Nuthatch can be coaxed onto a human hand, he will often take seed or nut meats while standing on a tree limb.*

On the sixth weekend, I decided it might be time to "land" a chick-adee. On this Saturday morning I carried yesterday's newspaper. Arriving at the gathering place, I sat down on the newspaper, to position my hand at ground level. I spread a dozen sunflower seeds on the ground two feet from my hand, which held several pieces of walnut meat. The chickadees were slow to arrive that morning; perhaps they were at the far end of their regular wanderings when I arrived. It was almost 20 minutes before I heard the first Black-caps approaching. A moment later the first chickadee to arrive flew to the ground beside me, selected a seed, and darted away. Within a minute, the rest of the group arrived and took up positions in the nearby shrubs. One by one they came to the ground, took a seed and flew off. Soon the only food available was in my left hand, resting on the ground. Now I would find out if these chickadees were ready to hand-feed. Several Black-caps landed nearby, searched for food on the ground, and flew up into the trees. I remained as motionless as possible, trying not even to blink. After what seemed like an hour (it was probably only five minutes) a Black-cap dropped down and landed an inch from my hand. He stood stock still, his head cocked to one side, looking directly at me.

Below: *Winning the confidence of a wild bird takes patience and a lot of gentle coaxing.*

*Right: Cheese crackers are high on the list of this White-breasted Nuthatch's preferred snacks.*

Sensing no threat, he hopped to my hand, reached over, took a seed and sped off. Close, I thought — let's see if he comes right back. Sure enough, in less than a minute this bird was back on the ground. Before he returned I lifted my hand several inches above ground level. With no hesitation, he jumped onto my hand, took a seed, and was gone.

My time that morning was up. I scattered the remaining food on the ground and walked back to my car.

It was now early February. My schedule did not allow consecutive visits that month and I wondered if a two-week interval would set the process back. When I returned to this state park, I repeated the events of two weeks before, with much success. The chickadees seemed at ease in my presence as I sat on the ground, seed in hand. In less than five minutes a single Black-cap was on my hand and, though I could not be sure, I suspect it was the same individual who had hand-fed two weeks earlier. The few seeds I placed on the ground nearby quickly disappeared, and finally a second chickadee began flying to my hand. Before a half hour had passed, at least four of the dozen or so chickadees were taking food from my hand.

On subsequent visits through the end of March, an increasing number of this band of chickadees began hand-feeding. It appeared to me that the more timid ones simply needed more time to break through their strong, instinctive wariness of a human.

When I went back to this state park the following October, I was more than a little curious to see if any of the hand-feeding chickadees would be in evidence. My concerns were quickly put to rest. Returning to the same feeding place, two chickadees were hand-feeding within 15 minutes of my appearance. I cannot prove it conclusively, but I believe they must have been a part of the little flock I got to know earlier that year. Two weekends later, five chickadees were busily hand-feeding soon after my entrance into the park. Birds have excellent memories. (You will see further evidence of this in Chapter 4 on chickadees.)

Using this same procedure (which I call "setting the table") I have brought, since that first trial several years ago with chickadees, many Tufted Titmice to the hand. This is not too surprising since titmice often travel with chickadees, and have much the same personality and temperament as their black-capped brethren. More recently, White-breasted and Red-breasted Nuthatches have come to my hand by means of "setting the table," and several other species have walked up to my hand for food, while not yet being willing to land directly on the hand.

*Above: A more aggressive Red-breasted Nuthatch succeeds in thwarting the attempts of the chickadee, on the right, in getting first choice from the handful of sunflower seeds and nut meats.*
*Right Page: It is never too young to begin the experience of hand-feeding wild birds. Alexis, the author's granddaughter at age 2, goes "eyeball to eyeball" with a friendly chickadee in a Massachusetts Sanctuary. Photo by Alexis' mother, Wendy Wiberg.*

# Chapter Four—Chickadees

## (and individual Black-caps I have known)

I remember quite clearly the first time I watched a Black-capped Chickadee fly down from a tree and perch on someone's hand. Although this incident happened almost 20 years ago, it is one of those special moments which will stay with me forever.

It happened north of Boston, in one of the several Massachusetts wildlife sanctuaries I occasionally visit. I had seen photos of Black-caps on a hand, but had never observed a "live" landing. Rounding a bend on a path that snowy December morning I saw, about 50 feet ahead, a lone figure standing quite still with his left hand extended. I stopped to watch, not at all sure what the man was doing. Soon, a chickadee darted out of the brush, flew to his hand for a seed, and sped quickly off. Fascinated, I watched for ten minutes as the scene repeated itself many times. Not wanting to disturb that peaceful scene, I turned and quietly retraced my steps.

I thought about that experience often the following week, and the next Sunday morning I went back to this sanctuary with a pocket full of sunflower seeds. Not knowing quite what to expect, I walked into the same area, filled my left hand with seeds and waited, arm extended. It was biting cold that day, and my hand soon began to ache. There was no sign of bird activity anywhere. I was all alone and starting to feel just a bit foolish, standing there with my hand held out and nothing happening. A man and woman walked by, and I quickly put my hand into my coat pocket until they passed, after exchanging quick "Hellos." I remember struggling with a sense of embarrassment, before I went looking again for my seeds.

*Left Page: Chickadees are likely to be your first subjects of hand-feeding. Here, one pauses proudly before feeding and fleeing. He was immediately followed by a procession of group members.*
*Below: A pair of chickadees having landed simultaneously, attempt to assert pecking order status.*

Exercising much patience (or stubbornness) I stuck with it for an hour, despite the biting cold. For whatever the reason, the only birds I saw that day were a couple of crows — not a peep from one chickadee. Disappointed, I continued with my walk and a half hour or so later, returned to my car. Not a promising start in my efforts to hand-feed a wild bird.

Several weeks later I went back to this sanctuary for another try. As luck would have it, the man I had watched feeding the chickadees earlier was there again and once more he had a steady stream of Black-caps taking sunflower seeds from his hand. This time, feeling a bit bolder and increasingly curious to learn what his secret was, I approached the man and we soon began chatting. He introduced himself as "Bob," a retired real estate agent who lived nearby. Bob, it turned out, took his exercise in this sanctuary once or twice a week, and had, over several years, developed a close kinship with many of the resident creatures, winged and otherwise. He was especially fond of hand-feeding "his" chickadees.

During this second meeting, Bob encouraged me to stand beside him, seed in extended hand, while he fed the chickadees. He explained that a novice hand-feeder, in the company of someone the birds knew, would probably have success. There was no question in his mind that chickadees (and other species) do recognize individual humans and will come to them regularly once semi-tamed, after months and even years of separation. Within minutes of his invitation, much to my great pleasure, I had my very first Black-cap landing.

In the following weeks through my sporadic contacts with this gentleman, I learned much about the business of hand-feeding birds. Without question, my increasingly intensive interest in this activity (and later, photographing birds on the hand) stemmed from this accidental crossing of paths with my friend Bob. From time to time in our lives we meet people who seem to possess an inborn affinity with wild creatures. These exceptional individuals make quick and confident connections with wild birds and animals.

Here are the three key elements to remember when setting out to hand-feed birds, as conveyed to me in those initial conversations with Bob:

## Presence

Until the resident birds get to know you and feel comfortable with your presence, or you happen upon birds which have become accustomed to people hand-feeding them, it will be difficult to hand-feed chickadees.

## Motion

The absence of motion is critical. Always move very slowly, if movement is necessary. Birds instinctively regard sudden movements as a threat to their safety.

## Timing

There are certain times of the day and year, in combination with weather conditions, when your chances of success with hand-feeding increase dramatically. Perhaps the optimum time and conditions here in the northeast are November through February, between sunrise and 10:00 A.M., the day before and a day or two after a severe ice or snow storm.

If you ever succeed in hand-feeding a wild bird, chances are that your first such experience will be with a Black-capped Chickadee. I have carried on a love affair with these little bundles of black and white energy since that day, long past, when I first hand-fed a Black-cap. I would estimate that I have hand-fed several hundred individual chickadees in a variety of locations, including, of course, my own backyard.

Chickadees are among the very easiest of the woodland birds to semi-tame. Even so, a Black-cap which has never had contact with a human probably will not come to the hand at first. They must study you to gain confidence that you intend no harm.

Chickadees, to me, are the embodiment of cheerfulness, spunk, and joi de vivre! They are naturally inquisitive, they are wonderfully self-confident, and they are in perpetual motion. Whenever my spirits are low, I try to schedule a trip to a nearby sanctuary; these little woodland sprites never fail to pick me up. And, frequently, where there are chickadees, there will also be a couple of titmice, and two or three White- and Red-breasted Nuthatches.

What a marvelously engineered little bundle of energy a wintering-over bird is. The temperature may be near zero, the winter wind can be ferocious, yet the chickadees and their fellow travelers bounce through the trees and around our feeders as if it was spring! This always amazes me: somehow they manage to find enough sustenance on the ground and on the trees to survive our harsh northeast winters. A severe ice storm is about the only weather condition which can put a chickadee's existence in jeopardy. A coating of ice will cover up the insect eggs and larvae hidden in the bark of the trees and (you may have noticed) will cause increased activity at backyard feeders. This is an ideal time to experiment with hand-feeding. Birds have tiny furnaces: they will continue to function as long as fuel is available.

In winter, chickadees move through the woodlands in various-sized family groups on a more-or-less-regular route. I have seen flocks as large as 30 or 40 (they are hard to count since they are always in motion) and as small as two or three. Based on my observations, their winter-roving territory appears to be a rough circle perhaps 200 yards in diameter. I have noticed that these extended families tend to center their wanderings within 50 yards of an area which is frequented by visitors engaging in hand-feeding.

Inevitably, spring comes and the roving bands of chickadees begin to pair off. Their chic-a-dee-dee-dee call is heard less frequently by early April, and is replaced by a two-or-three note call which sounds like fee-bee or fee-bee-bee. The first note is the longest; what follows is a full tone lower. Their personalities seem to change also. They appear less interested in associating with humans, as their instinctive attention turns to mating and finding nesting sites. Food slowly becomes more available as the season warms and this is another reason why hand-feeding is usually confined to late fall, winter, and early spring. I rarely hand-feed from May through September.

Have you ever wondered why you have never seen a baby chickadee tagging along with its parents? In June or July, the female lays her five to ten eggs in a tiny nest usually found in a rotting birch or pine tree. Often the nests have been abandoned by woodpeckers—otherwise the pair of

chickadees excavate their own little chambers, about the size and volume of a coffee cup. Nesting material is composed of a mix of feathers, grass, fur, and whatever else is soft and available. The eggs hatch in ten to twelve days and the fledglings begin their constant demand for food. Now begins the busiest time of the year for the parents, and they have to scramble for food from dawn to dusk to satisfy their brood. Just three weeks after hatching and while still in their nests, the youngsters are nearly as large as their parents, which explains why we will probably never see a half-or three-quarter-sized chickadee. Bird watchers here in the northeast are at their most active from April through June, which further

*Above: A dominant, Red-breasted Nuthatch on right, delivers a warning to the submissive chickadee on the left.*

decreases the likelihood of observing less than full-sized chickadees when the young leave their nests in July. By the end of September the juveniles, now three-or-four months old, are fully grown and are pretty much fending for themselves. At this stage of their development, it is close to impossible to differentiate this year's brood from older birds.

Depending on a variety of factors, Black-caps may live for five to eight years in the wild. Occasionally, you will read of a banded bird which is reported to be 10-or 11-years old, but this is not typical. I hand-fed one chickadee with a distinguishing physical characteristic for five winters before he (or she) failed to reappear in October of 1990. More about "Peg Leg" later in this chapter.

*Above: A pair of chickadees take turns feeding from the hand.*

Some species of birds are more acrobatic than others. High on the list of avian stunt men is the chickadee. It is said that a Black-cap in flight can change direction in 3/100 of a second. I witnessed an impressive example of this amazing quickness in my backyard several winters ago. I was offering sunflower seeds to the resident flock of chickadees early one winter morning. Down came a Black-cap, and as he landed, he accidentally kicked a seed off the edge of my hand. In a twinkling, this chickadee did a rollover, dove, and caught the seed about a foot above the ground. Yes, there were more seeds on my hand, but this little guy wanted that seed, for whatever reason.

It is interesting to observe the pecking order which exists in a flock of chickadees. There is a definite hierarchy in these extended families, and nowhere is this more evident than during hand-feeding in an area where the birds are familiar with the feeders. When a human appears in the neighborhood where Black-caps are moving though the shrubbery, they will often take-up a position in the surrounding trees and shrubs, awaiting their turn. One by one they come take a seed or nut, and fly off. They never descend in a group; it is always a case of "wait your turn." Rarely, two chickadees (who may have a similar place in the hierarchy) will land together. When this happens, the most aggressive of the two will lean toward the second bird with beak wide open, flex its wings in an aggressive manner, and emit a throaty hissing sound. This threatening action invariably chases the subordinate bird away, to await his or her proper turn.

Speaking of "his or her," I have often wished that I could tell the difference between male and female chickadees. This is not possible for me since their size and markings appear to be identical.

A part of the pleasure I experience from hand-feeding Black-capped chickadees is the ongoing hunt for those with unique markings or physical differences. Finding such a bird enables me to track it, to observe its

Below: A Black-capped Chickadee and a Tufted Titmouse share a hand of nut meats as each eyes the other cautiously.

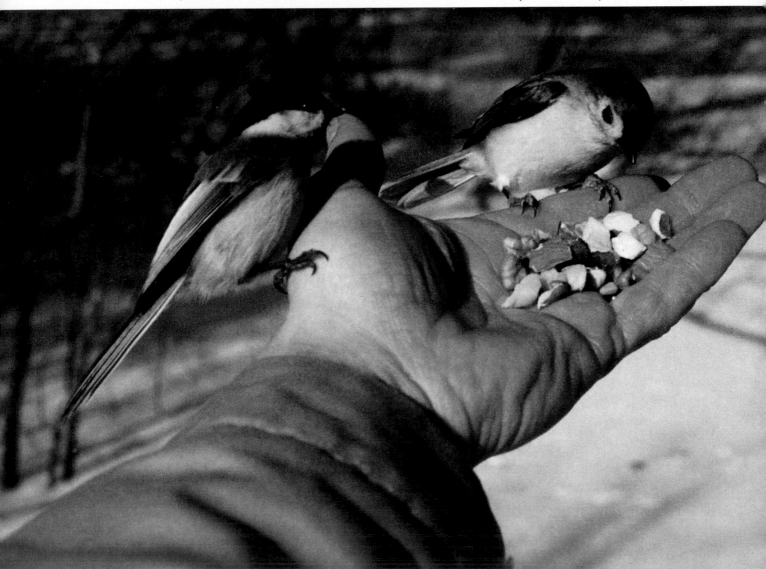

wanderings, and its life span. Each time a chickadee lands, I look to see if there is something different about it. Ninety-nine times out of a hundred there is not. In the hundreds of Black-caps I have observed at a distance of 20 inches, I have seen only five which were not clones of the rest of the population.

## Stub Tail

The first different chickadee came to my hand about 15 years ago in Topsfield, Massachusetts. As he approached, I knew immediately there was something unusual about him. (Since I never knew the sex of the following individuals, I choose, for simplicities' sake, and for no sexist reason, to refer to each of them as he, because he precedes she in the alphabet!) This bird's approach resembled the flight of a drunken Goldfinch as it bobbed erratically up and down in a decidedly un-chickadee manner. When he paused briefly on my index finger, I quickly understood the problem. Instead of a normal two-inch tail, this fellow showed only a quarter-inch of tail. My speculation is that he may have lost his tail to a turtle or a snake or a bird of prey. Otherwise, Stub Tail seemed quite average, and I could not see that his taillessness was adversely affecting him. I would smile as I saw him coming toward me that winter, in his herky, jerky way. Toward the end of winter, I thought I noticed that his tail was longer. I was told later by an experienced birder that birds will regenerate their tail feathers within a year if they lose them. When I returned the following fall to this sanctuary, I wondered if Stub Tail would reappear. He did not, at least in his former tailless state. I suspect that I probably did see him again that next winter, with his new tail feathers fully in place.

## Limper

I met this fellow late in the fall of 1978. He appeared in the company of a group of 15 or so chickadees in a sand pit area I visit in North Wilmington, Massachusetts close to the North Reading town line. The chickadees in that area knew me (and still do), so I would always put some sunflower seed or nut meats in a pocket before setting off. Several minutes after entering the path leading into the sand pits, the little band of Black-caps spotted me and flew directly over. One by one they came to my hand until it appeared that everyone had come down at least once. After a pause of a minute or two, a straggler landed on my left thumb. Usually when a chickadee lands, you feel a solid two-claw grip. This time it was different and the reason was quickly obvious. This bird's left claw, though seemingly complete, did not grip when he landed. His demeanor seemed subdued, as though somehow he was not really with it. Otherwise, Limper seemed normal physically, and I have no idea why that left claw would not clench when he landed. He was with this band of chickadees all of that fall and winter, and when I returned in November of 1979 he was there to greet me. During that time Limper and his companions were never more than 100 yards from the spot where I first met them. In February of 1980 he disappeared. Perhaps he was already old when I first saw him in 1978, and he probably met his demise during that unusually severe winter.

## White Spot

This Black-cap had a tiny white spot just above his right eye. It looked as though someone had touched him with an artist's paint brush. Otherwise, he was no different than the dozen other chickadees he travelled with in the Ipswich River Wildlife Sanctuary. I first met White Spot about mid-winter of 1986. I hand-fed him in the company of his merry band for three winters. April of 1988 was our last contact; when I returned in the late fall of 1988 he was nowhere to be seen.

## Clubfoot

I am not sure that there is any special significance that three of these five "special" chickadees had problems relating to their claws. Clubfoot, first encountered in my back yard in 1987, had a normal right claw, while its left claw was clenched in a permanent knot. When he landed on my hand, that club-shaped foot acted as a balance while he selected a seed. Since he was always close to my home, I tended to hand-feed him year 'round, as I felt he probably needed a little extra help. Mostly though, since there are bird feeders in the neighborhood, I just wanted to maintain contact with him because he was different. I last saw Clubfoot early in March of 1991. One day he simply was not with his group of about ten chickadees. I had seen a northern shrike in the nearby woods that winter, and I have wondered if its presence may have accounted for Clubfoot's sudden absence.

## Peg Leg

I think I must have met Peg Leg when he was about six months old. It was on a clear, crisp October morning in Topsfield in 1985 that we first studied each other at arm's length. There he stood on my hand, noticeably smaller than the other chickadees in his extended family, and seeming quite tentative. It was his slight build and reticent manner which suggested to me that he was probably born early that summer. His left claw was not there at all; the leg was complete right to the point where his claw should have been. When he landed, the footless leg, as a balance, stabilized him while his right claw secured a strong grip. What I did not realize at this first meeting was that this would become the beginning of a special, extended friendship.

I suspect that there are "runts of the litter" in the world of birds, as is the case in most other multiple birth creatures. Peg Leg was probably one, since he never measured up in size, with his brothers and sisters. The average chickadee weighs one third of an ounce. I doubt that this fellow weighed more than one quarter ounce. What he lacked in size, he compensated for in spunk. Although he was tentative with me in the beginning, he was soon sure of his safety in my presence, and I could count on seeing and feeding him every time I visited the sanctuary.

There was always the possibility that Peg Leg lost his left claw to a predator, yet I always had the feeling that this was a birth defect. I fed Peg Leg weekly for the next five months, until April of 1986 arrived and I turned my attention to getting the peas planted. Often that summer I wondered if this little guy would be there to greet me in October.

On a blustery late October morning, I went to that sanctuary with Peg Leg very much on my mind. Sure enough, within 15 minutes there he was, traveling with a large group of Black-caps. In the pecking order, he was well toward the end, confirming my suspicion that he was a juvenile. His first landing that day is especially clear to me. Suddenly he appeared on my index finger, stock still. His head was cocked to one side and he stared silently at me for several seconds as if to say, "Well, where have you been these past six months?!" Finally, he picked up a seed and flew off. Peg Leg was a regular visitor that winter, along with his large extended family.

By the end of that second winter, Peg Leg had begun to accompany me, sometimes perched on my shoulder, as I walked around the sanctuary. I cannot explain why a special bond had developed between us, but there was no mistaking that it existed. I have wondered if this bird might have been semi-ostracized by his companions because he was a runt with

*Below: A subservient chickadee at left awaits its turn to feed.*

one claw. In any event, Peg Leg spent more time with me when I was in that sanctuary than did any of his companions. In spite of that, since occasionally I would miss the weekend visit to Topsfield due to other commitments, there was no indication that he was dependent on me for sustenance. When I was not around, Peg Leg did what chickadees are programmed to do: he found his food on and in the trees and shrubs along his regular travel route.

The years slipped by and Peg Leg never missed visiting me during my weekend walks. Invariably, he was on my hand and shoulder within ten minutes of my arrival at the sanctuary. This fellow truly was my little pet, in a way that none of the other chickadees ever were.

Our first contact had been in October of 1985 and the last time I saw him was in March of 1990. When I said good-by to Peg Leg early in the spring of 1990 I fully expected to see him again the following October. That was not to be. It was mid-November before I returned to Peg Leg's neighborhood. An hour went by that morning and, although I encountered several wandering flocks of chickadees, there was no sign of my little pal. I never saw him again and the feeling of sadness at his disappearance was very strong. He probably did not perish from old age since he was only five years old. My surmise is that he came to the end of his life because of a predator. There are many natural enemies of small birds in any sanctuary, including hawks, owls, turtles, foxes, and snakes. I do miss my little friend. Maybe some day I will find another Peg Leg.

I regret that I have no photos of any of these specific chickadees. It was not until October of 1990 that I began seriously photographing birds on my hand, as you will learn in Chapter 9.

Below: Which Black-capped Chickadee will back off? In this instance, the bird at the right was dominant, as the other black-cap flew off to await its rightful turn.

# Chapter Five—Tufted Titmice

It is impossible to convey, even with a well-focused, close-up photograph, the true beauty of this charming bird.

The first time I observed a Tufted Titmouse was in 1976. When I spotted it at our Wilmington bird feeder that winter, I could not immediately identify it. *Peterson's Eastern Field Guide* quickly introduced me to this newcomer to our backyard.

Although Tufted Titmice sightings have been noted very occasionally in New England since the 1920s and 1930s, their numbers here in the extreme northeast have been very limited until recently. It was not until the mid-1970s that this bird expanded its range north into Connecticut and Massachusetts, along with Cardinals and Mockingbirds. As this book is written (1993), titmice are regular feeder visitors as far north as central Vermont and New Hampshire. It is not known for certain what changing conditions are responsible for this expansion. Two possible explanations are a moderating winter trend over the last quarter century and a great proliferation of backyard bird feeders. Birds tend to move into areas where they can count on a steady supply of food.

As with chickadees, it is not possible to differentiate a male from a female titmouse, although based on my observations, I suspect that the males may be slightly larger and more aggressive than the females.

A distinguishing field mark is the titmouse's beady black eyes, which stand out sharply against its mostly grayish feathers.

When spring arrives, titmice become quite vocal. Their loud peter peter peter, repeated monotonously for what can seem like hours, rings through the trees and shrubs throughout the nesting season. By the end of June, their "peters" are heard much less frequently. Titmice

*Right: This titmouse paused for a fleeting second before carrying his morsel off to a nearby tree.*

nests are found in hollows of trees and are lined with moss and other soft materials.

Five to seven eggs hatch in May or June and the following summer months are a constant scramble for enough insects and seed to feed the brood. Since titmice do not migrate, they will continue to use their spring and summer nests during the winter as protection from the icy winds.

During the months from October though March you are likely to see several Tufted Titmice in the company of chickadees, nuthatches, Downy Woodpeckers, and once in a while a Brown Creeper.

Until five or six years ago, I was unaware that titmice could be encouraged to hand-feed. I will not soon forget the first time a Tufted Titmouse landed on my hand for a sunflower seed.

Below: A titmouse is "caught" in the instant before flying-off with a bit of nut meat.

On a crisp Sunday morning that January, I was standing near a frozen pond in a Massachusetts wildlife sanctuary hand-feeding the resident chickadees. There had been a classic midwinter snowstorm the week before, and there was nearly a foot of snow on the ground. With the temperature hovering around 15 degrees, conditions were perfect for hand-feeding.

I had casually observed for many winters that titmice travel with Black-caps. Titmice always seemed interested in watching the chickadees flitting back and forth to my hand, but it had not seriously crossed my mind that one would land on a human's hand. This bird simply appeared to have a much stronger wariness of humans compared with chickadees.

The closest I had been to a Tufted Titmouse was when I accidentally dropped a bit of food on the ground and then watched as a titmouse darted in, picked up the morsel, and scooted quickly away.

On this morning, there must have been 30 chickadees availing themselves of seeds and nut meats. Due to the heavy snow cover which made ground feeding impossible, the Black-caps were much more active than usual. As soon as a Black-cap left my hand, another would land. More often than usual, two Black-caps would land simultaneously, often resulting in a brief pecking-order confrontation. Nearly an hour went by, and the intense cold was beginning to penetrate my several layers of clothing. I was about ready to turn and retrace my steps to the car when it happened. There, standing stock still on my nearly frozen index finger, was a Tufted Titmouse! What impressed me was that he was not the least bit intimidated in my presence. The crest on a titmouse will lie flattened to the head when the bird is alarmed or frightened. This bird's crest was

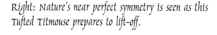
*Right: Nature's near perfect symmetry is seen as this Tufted Titmouse prepares to lift-off.*

standing straight up as he looked me over. He appeared to have no fear of me. After several seconds, he took a piece of walnut and flew to a nearby pine tree. I watched as he devoured his snack. With no hesitation he came directly back to my hand for seconds. By now I had completely forgotten that my hand was a piece of ice, and I was ready to remain in that spot as long as this bird continued to hand-feed. Perhaps ten minutes later, after seven or eight visits, the titmouse departed and I walked quickly back to the car.

It is possible, of course, that this bird had previously hand-fed. Although I will never know for certain, I believe that this titmouse was simply carried away by the frenzy of activity created by the chickadees.

On successive weekends, that single titmouse came to my hand regularly. I could tell for a near certainty that this was the same bird by his immediate presence in that area, and by his most confident demeanor. None of the several other titmice in that neighborhood could be coaxed to my hand that winter. This single bird, nicknamed Tom (just because "Tom Titmouse" sounded appropriate) was a regular hand feeder the ensuing three winters, after which he disappeared.

*Left: A titmouse eyes the buffet before making his choice and quickly departing.*

Three winters ago, I set out to see if Tom was just a very rare exception to the rule. I wondered if other titmice would hand-feed, using the table setting approach described in Chapter 3. I conducted this test in a nearby rock and sand quarry within distance of my home in Wilmington, Massachusetts. I visit this spot often from October through March because there is an unusually large flock of chickadees living here, ready and willing to hand-feed. I can always count on lots of feathered company during these early morning walks, and it was here that I met and got to know "Limper," described in Chapter 4. Titmice are quite common in this neighborhood, as are finches, jays, nuthatches, Downy Woodpeckers, Cardinals, a Mockingbird or two, and assorted sparrows.

I found a convenient clearing at the edge of the quarry and decided that this would be a fine place to set the table. For three consecutive Saturday mornings, I scattered a mix of seeds, nut meats and bread crusts on the ground 20 feet from a boulder on which I sat. Predictably, in less than five minutes there appeared the usual band of Black-caps, who were, after several winters, quite comfortable with my presence. Many of these chickadees came directly to my hand for food, even though there was a very visible and plentiful supply on the ground nearby. Before I left on that third Saturday, I noted the visitors who were taking food as follows:

| | |
|---|---|
| chickadees | 30 (best estimate) |
| Blue Jays | 4 |
| White-throated Sparrows | 4 |
| Titmice | 4 |
| House Finches | 3 |
| White-breasted Nuthatches | 2 |
| Mockingbird | 1 |
| Cardinal | 1 |

I had seen two Red-breasted Nuthatches the week before, but they were not present on this third visit.

*Right: Before selecting a bit of nut meat, this titmouse paused a brief moment, to study the photographer.*

On the fourth Saturday morning I proceeded as before, but shortened the distance between myself and the feeding spot. I sat down on an old cushion 10 feet away and waited. Soon the chickadees appeared, first two, then three or four, and finally the entire vanguard. Some came directly to my hand, the rest went to the table nearby. In nature, a crowd tends to attract a crowd. Soon I became aware that finches and titmice were moving in, taking up positions in the nearby shrubbery. Where there was no hesitation on the part of the chickadees, there was some understandable reluctance on the part of the latecomers to dive in. Even though I sat rock still, the titmice and finches were cautious.

For several minutes the chickadees were the only birds feeding. Then a Tufted Titmouse flew down to the table, took a piece of walnut and flew off. A minute later, this same titmouse was back for more. Two other tit-mice perched close by soon flew over and began feeding. I was careful not to move a muscle. I am sure that these titmice overcame their hesitancy of a man sitting nearby by observing the non-stop feeding activity of the Black-caps. During the ensuing half hour none of the several other kinds of birds who were watching from close by would come to the ground while I was that close. As I was walking away, I turned to see several Blue Jays, White-throats, finches and sparrows moving in for breakfast.

By the sixth Saturday, I was sitting just a yardstick away from the ground food. This proximity, as usual, made absolutely no difference to the chickadees. They were buzzing me and the nearby food as though I was one of the family. It did take several minutes longer for the titmice to join in, but in less than ten minutes they had joined the chickadees and were feeding on the ground. They had now become acclimated to my presence at arm's length. I repeated this scenario with the same results the following weekend.

On the eighth Saturday morning I did not scatter seed and nuts on the ground. Instead, sitting on my cushion yoga fashion, I extended both seed-laden hands, offering the usual fare. In seconds, the first chickadees were coming and going and in a very few minutes the rest of the resident Black-caps were present. My only motion was to replenish the seeds in my hands as needed. This was done v-e-r-y slowly, so as not to scare the pair of titmice who had been sitting on a limb nearby. I thought "Alright fellows, will you come to my hand this morning?"

Fifteen minutes went by and the Black-caps were having their usual busy picnic. It seemed to me that the titmice were simply waiting for me to scatter a few seeds on the ground, at which point they would surely join the fun. I would not budge, and neither would the titmice. To try to end the stalemate, I dropped several bits of seed just to the front. Immediately, one of the titmice flew down, picked up a bit of nutmeat and was off. The second tufted flew down soon after. They proceeded to pick food off the ground for several minutes, but would not yet come to my hand after the ground food had disappeared.

Next week, maybe.

It all came together on the ninth Saturday. My only change in strategy (once again not spreading food on the ground) was to lower my left hand to ground level, while keeping my right hand in my pocket. At once the Black-caps were darting on and off my hand. Three titmice soon appeared, and quickly one of them came to the ground six inches from my hand. He stood there for a minute or so, watching the chickadees buzzing in and out. Then, cautiously, he hopped over and, still on the ground, reached in to select a seed. Off he went to eat his morsel. A second tit-mouse came down, landed a foot away, and looked at me as if to say, "Hey, let's have some seeds over here!" While he stood there the first tit-mouse came back, landed beside my hand, took food, and flew away. Ever so tentatively, the second bird hopped over, took a seed and shot away.

At that point I filled my right hand with food and resumed feeding the chickadees from both hands, now well above ground level. The chickadees were landing nonstop; as soon as one bird left, another arrived. I kept an eye on the three titmice, wondering if one of them would finally fly to my hand. Finally — at last! The apparent leader of the little band of titmice flew to my left hand. His crest was flattened on his head, indicating some fear and trepidation. He snatched a seed and flew back to his companions. A minute later he was right back, this time, it seemed, with less hesitancy. This individual continued to hand-feed for ten minutes, and all the while the other two barely moved.

Finally, feeling the cold, I stood up, scattered the remaining food on the ground and walked away.

Before the end of March, two of those three titmice were landing quickly on my hand along with the chickadees. The third bird always waited for food to be dropped on the ground.

This winter (1992-1993) I have been hand-feeding five Tufted Titmice at this location, and I suspect (though I cannot prove it) that two of the five are the originals who first dared to land on my hand three winters ago.

*Right: A Tufted Titmouse makes a tentative landing. Crest down on head indicates this bird is not relaxed and at ease.*

The question can be asked — is it worth spending an hour or so for nine or ten weekend mornings to eventually coax a Tufted Titmouse onto the hand? It certainly will not be for very many people, I suspect. It was for me, since I combined my desire for the health benefits of a two-mile walk with the great pleasure of looking into the eyes of a titmouse at a distance of 18 inches.

# Chapter Six—White-Breasted Nuthatch

Big, bold and curious — that might be an appropriate description of the White-breasted Nuthatch.

With the exception of the southern half of Florida, this common nuthatch is a familiar woodland and backyard species, its range spreading north and easterly across the Canadian maritime provinces. If you have ever taken a walk into a mature forest, you have probably heard the familiar yank call of this bird.

My mother used to refer to her white-breasted visitors as the "Upside-down bird." She knew the proper name, but preferred to use this nickname.

This larger of our two eastern nuthatches, seemingly always on the move, can be seen on large tree trunks and main limbs, scrabbling down and around the tree in its constant search for food. Insect eggs and insects in other stages of metamorphosis make up a large part of the White-breasted Nuthatch's diet. Although we may think of this bird as primarily an insect eater, its diet is far ranging, and actually inclines more toward the vegetarian side. Acorns, beechnuts, wild filberts, along with a wide selection of berries and other fruits, constitute the bulk of its diet. If there are bird feeders containing sunflower seeds within 200 yards of their home territory, White-breasted Nuthatches will soon discover them. In my hand-feeding efforts, I have learned that this larger of our two native nuthatches is especially fond of cheese crackers and bits of walnuts and almonds.

At our house, we count the White-breasted Nuthatches among our regular backyard visitors. Unlike the chickadees, who sometimes swarm to the feeders, we rarely see more than two nuthatches at a time. One reason for this is that nuthatches simply are not as commonly found in our woods as are some of the other species. Another reason is that these birds are extremely territorial. They do not congregate in extended families as Black-caps often do. The only time I have seen more than two or three White-breasts traveling together has been in June and July, when the parent birds are still looking after the fledglings. By September and October, the young have been fully weaned and are off on their own, staking out new territories.

As with the other species of birds I have succeeded in hand-feeding, my efforts with White-breasted Nuthatches are limited to the months from November through March. As mentioned earlier, attempts at hand-feeding during the warmth of spring and summer have been noticeably less productive, since there is then a plentiful supply of easy-to-find insects, nuts, and berries. Further, the adults are so busy late spring and summer rearing their young that they do not seem interested in associating with humans.

According to most bird-guide books, the only way to tell a male from a female White-breasted Nuthatch is to look closely at the top of the head. This is difficult, certainly, at a distance of 20 or 30 feet, but very easy at

*Left Page: A White-breasted Nuthatch, with a quizzical look, hesitates a moment before taking a sunflower seed.*

18 inches. The crown of the male is jet black, while the female's crown appears more grayish black. As far as I can see, this is the only color difference with nuthatches (including Red-breasts); however, there seems also to be a slight difference between the sexes in size. From what I have observed, the males may be slightly larger than their mates, by perhaps ten percent.

In the five or six years since I first hand-fed a White-breasted Nuthatch, I have been successful with no more than a half-dozen individuals. One of them, a male I call "Black Bart," lives in an eastern Massachusetts wildlife sanctuary, and has been taking seeds and nut meats from my hand for five winters. Black Bart is alive and well (spring 1993), and I see him and hand-feed him two or three times a month, November through April. Hopefully he will be there waiting for me when I return to his territory next November. I will relate how I brought Black Bart to my hand later in this chapter.

Another reason why I have fed comparatively few White-breasts is because, compared with chickadees, they are very reluctant by nature to put themselves into such intimate proximity with humans. It takes much longer, perhaps ten times longer, to bring a wild White-breasted Nuthatch to the hand than it does with a chickadee. Most of us, unless we have won the lottery or are retired, will not have the time required to semi-tame more than one or two White-breasted Nuthatches. In my experience, (unless one happens to cross paths with an individual bird which has already learned to hand-feed), it takes from eight to a dozen or more visits to a location where you have found nuthatches before a hand-landing can be achieved. If you are not blessed with an abundance of patience, I would recommend that you stick with Black-capped Chickadees!

Left: Occasionally two birds will arrive at the hand at the same moment. The chickadee on the right, flew off immediately when he spotted the larger, more aggressive nuthatch.

Until the winter of 1987-1988, I was not aware that White-breasted Nuthatches could be encouraged to hand-feed. On a cold and blustery December morning in 1987, I was visiting a nearby sanctuary, combining the need to take my every other day two-mile walk with hand-feeding chickadees and titmice. I had taken a position near a picturesque little pond, and the Black-caps were darting about in great numbers. After a while a White-breasted Nuthatch caught my attention with its persistent yank-yank call. He was working his way, headfirst as always, down a huge oak tree about 20 yards away. I kept an eye on him, because he seemed to be half watching the activity taking place around me. Over a period of ten minutes or so, he slowly approached, the better to see what this business with the chickadees was all about. Eventually he sat near the end of an overhanging branch perhaps ten feet over my head. This was closer then I had ever been to a White-breasted Nuthatch. I stayed at this spot for another 15 or 20 minutes, feeding the Black-caps, and quietly studying the observer overhead. The nuthatch appeared content to just sit and watch. Finally, the cold was taking its toll on my hands and I decided it was time to leave. I scattered a handful of hulled sunflower seeds on the ground and walked away. Turning to look back from a short way up the path, I watched as the nuthatch dropped to the ground. Since the sunflower seeds had no shells, he consumed several immediately, then began stashing the rest behind chunks of bark in nearby trees. When the last seed was gone, he flew off and I walked back to the warmth of the car.

*Right: His snack secure in his beak, "Black Bart" (referred to earlier in the text) prepares to fly-off to hide his morsel behind some loose bark on a nearby tree.*

The following weekend I drove back to this same sanctuary, and proceeded into the general area I had visited the week before. As usual, the chickadees were very much in evidence, the day was sunny and a bit warmer, and I listened for the familiar nattering of any nearby nuthatches. Then, with no warning, a single White-breasted Nuthatch flew into the area and landed on the trunk of a nearby pine tree. We looked each other over and, although I could not be certain, I sensed that this was my friend from last weekend. The chickadees were busy, darting on and off my hands. I stayed stock still, trying to imitate a backyard feeder, hoping to encourage the nuthatch to come near. Although he approached to within 10 to 12 feet, he would not venture closer. He did appear to be quite interested in viewing the steady stream of chickadees who were availing themselves of free sunflower seeds. It was time for me to return home for dinner.

Over the ensuing weekends as my schedule allowed, I visited this same sanctuary, gradually gaining confidence that eventually this nuthatch would come to my hand. There was no longer any doubt in my mind that he recognized me and was becoming comfortable with my presence. Within a few minutes of my taking a position in his territory, he, and sometimes a second White-breast which I assumed was his mate, would appear. My perseverance was soon to be rewarded.

Late that winter, I decided it was time to find out if this nuthatch was ready to hand-feed. I stood that day beside a five-foot stump of a sycamore tree. Holding several pieces of nut meat, I placed my hand on the tree stump as soon as I spotted my friend watching from a nearby tree. The chickadees were very busy that day; fortunately I had a deep pocket full of hulled sunflower seeds and nut meats. The White-breasted Nuthatch finally flew over to a lilac shrub three or four feet from my hand on the tree stump. There he sat, watching the chickadees coming and going. Finally, he summoned his courage, and flew over to the top of the stump, several inches from my hand. Ever so slowly he walked up to my fingers, reached over, and, still on the stump, selected a bit of food. Up he flew to a nearby tree where he proceeded to devour his morsel. Back he came, and this time, without hesitation he landed beside my hand and helped himself again. After a dozen or so trips, I withdrew my hand from the stump and stood back. The nuthatch landed on the stump, hesitated a few seconds and flew onto my hand. To reinforce his increasing sense of confidence, I stayed for some time as he returned again and again. Now he was storing food behind loose bark on nearby trees.

I continued to hand-feed him through mid-April, when my attention turned to the backyard vegetable garden. When I returned to that sanctuary six months later, there was no sign of this fellow. I have no idea what may have happened to him. I will speculate that either he was on in years when our paths crossed, or he fell victim to a predator over the summer and fall.

The following winter (December 1988), I set out to bring another White-breasted Nuthatch to my hand. This time I wanted to see if the setting the table approach described in Chapter 3 might prove to take less time than my previous effort. It was then that I made the acquaintance of Black Bart.

Along a secluded path in a Massachusetts wildlife sanctuary there is a two-foot stone wall which lends itself beautifully to sitting and watching. This low wall is about 12 feet long. On moderate winter days, especially on an occasional week day when the human foot traffic is light, it is a most pleasant experience to scatter bits of bread, crackers, nut meats and sunflower seed on one end of the wall, then sit quietly at the other end to await the inevitable company. Almost magically, the motionless human observer gradually seems to disappear, and the birds move in. First the chickadees come, two or three, then a half dozen are flitting back and forth. A Tufted Titmouse lands, takes a piece of cheese cracker and flies to an overhanging branch. The mix of birds which soon follows may consist of White- and Red-breasted Nuthatches, White-throated Sparrows, a Blue Jay or two, an occasional Downy Woodpecker, and a pair of Cardinals. If the human observer remains quite still, it is not unusual for eight or ten species of birds to appear in such surroundings within 15 or 20 minutes. The single small problem I have encountered in these ses-

*Right: A friendly red squirrel enjoys a bite of lunch at a "table" set to attract wild birds. This photo was taken at a distance of 4 feet.*

sions is with red squirrels, which are much more at ease in human company than are gray squirrels. If a family of red squirrels happens to be around when you have set the table, they will quickly find the food. If you attempt to shoo them away, it will impede your success in bringing the birds in. What I have done in such cases is scatter bread and crackers on the ground up the path a way. As often as not the red squirrels will go to the food a little further away from a human.

That winter, I visited this spot by the low stone wall on most Saturday or Sunday mornings. I had in mind to land at least one White-breasted Nuthatch and one Cardinal before spring. I came close with the Cardinal (See chapter 9) and was successful with two White-breasted Nuthatches.

By the third visit to the stone wall, a pair of White-breasts were appearing at the table regularly. The larger of the two, with its coal-black crown, was, I'm sure, the male. His mate sometimes accompanied him, and sometimes did not. They obviously lived in that area because the male regularly appeared for his handouts within five minutes of my arrival.

In succeeding visits, I slowly decreased the space between myself at one end of the wall, and the bits of food I was setting out at the far end. As usual, it made no difference at all to the chickadees if the food was 12 feet away, or six inches away. It was not long — perhaps a half-dozen visits — before the other species mentioned earlier were feeding quite comfortably at a distance of three or four feet, with the exception of the Cardinals and Downy Woodpeckers. They would come no closer than eight to ten feet.

I named the male White-breasted Nuthatch "Black Bart," solely for the fact that the crown of his head was as jet black as I had ever seen on a nuthatch.

By mid-winter he was walking confidently across the wall to within a foot or two of where I sat. From there it was just a short time until, while standing on the wall, he was taking food from my hand. In another couple of weeks I was lifting my hand above the wall and Black Bart was soon hand-feeding regularly.

His mate, sometimes visible on a surrounding tree, was never the least bit predisposed to coming closer to me than the far end of the stone wall. After Bart had ingested several bits of crackers or nut meats, he would proceed to stash food in crevices of bark on the surrounding trees until I left the area.

Over the intervening winters, I could absolutely count on meeting Black Bart every time I visited his backyard. I cannot say that I became attached to him (or he to me) in the same way that Peg Leg, the chickadee, and I knew each other, but there was, and still is, a kinship between us nevertheless.

Like all other nuthatches, Bart is an incurable hoarder. If there is excess food available, Black Bart and all of the other nuthatches I have met will tirelessly stay with the task of hiding the snack foods away for another day. I have never seen this species store food anywhere other than behind a chink of bark on a tree trunk or limb, while chickadees and titmice will almost always hide their excess seeds on the ground, under a leaf or in a tuft of grass.

Two winters ago, out of curiosity, I decided one Sunday morning to see just how long Black Bart would continue hoarding seeds and nut meats. I carried a standard size lunch bag filled with hulled sunflower seeds and broken pieces of walnuts that day, and sure enough, my friend was on my hand within minutes of walking into his territory. I was ready to stay and hand-feed for three hours, if necessary. Most of the food was carried off, as expected, by the usual crowd of chickadees and titmice who were in attendance that morning. Nevertheless, I thought I had enough provisions to outlast Bart's interest and energy. By my actual count, this White-breasted Nuthatch landed on my hand 128 times in a period of two-and-a-half hours. As fast as he could, Bart would take a seed or piece of walnut, fly to a nearby tree to stash his booty, and return to my hand. He was still coming and going when about 35 chickadees finally finished off the last of the food I had brought.

I do not know how long he would have continued that game if the food had not run out. I wonder also what percentage of the nuts he stored away he would personally, eventually, consume. Probably less than half, but that is just a guess.

Five years after the acclimation process was completed, I am still in fairly regular contact with Black Bart. When I visit this sanctuary he is always there, and he will swoop right in to hand-feed with me. Since nuthatches can live eight to ten years in the wild, I hope to continue this acquaintance for another several years.

*Right Page: There is great wonderment in hand-feeding wild birds. Here, both child and bird share the wonder.*
*Photo by Wendy Wiberg.*

# Chapter Seven—Red-Breasted Nuthatch

Each of the many and varied wild birds in our backyards and woodlands possess their own unique beauty.

There are several birds here in New England I never tire of viewing, either through my binoculars or close up on my hand. My binocular favorites are Golden-crowned Kinglets, Yellowthroats, White-throated Sparrows, and, when I can locate them, Pileated Woodpeckers. (I see Pileateds fairly often around Great Bay, near Portsmouth, New Hampshire.) Of the hand-feeding birds, my most favored are Tufted Titmice and Red-breasted Nuthatches.

Until the winter of 1988-1989, the closest I had been to a Red-breasted Nuthatch was perhaps 15 feet, near the backyard feeder. It had not occurred to me that this striking little bird could be coaxed onto a human hand.

Left Page: A Red-breasted Nuthatch pauses a for a moment before selecting a bit of nut meat.
Right: A Tufted Titmouse, on the left, is driven off by an aggressive Red-breasted Nuthatch who seems to be suggesting "first come, first served".

Before describing the two ways I have used in getting this smaller of the two nuthatches to land on my hand, let me tell you something about this charming bird. You will probably never see more than two or three Red-breasts at a time. The most I have ever observed traveling together was four, several winters ago at a nearby sanctuary. Over a three-month span by means of weekend visits, two of the four were regularly taking sunflower seeds or bits of mixed nuts from my hand. The other two would watch and approach to about four feet, but could not be encouraged to hand-feed.

Red-breasted Nuthatches are not true migrators. They do not, like American Robins and Red-winged Blackbirds, fly south in late September to return like clockwork in March. This tiny nuthatch sometimes remains in one location year around or, more likely, will spend spring and summer in the pine woods of Canada, and fall and winter scattered throughout the United States. In years when the Canadian pine cone crop fails or is poor, we will see more Red-breasts retreating south to our American woods and, if we are lucky, showing up around our backyard feeders. We ordinarily do not think of this bird as one of our regular visitors as we do with chickadees, titmice, and goldfinches.

Unlike chickadees, it is possible, though difficult, to differentiate male from female Red-breasted Nuthatches. In size they are identical but the coloring at the top of the head, or crown, is different. In the male, the crown is jet black while the female's is a lighter, grayish-black. It takes a keen eye to tell the difference, though at a distance of 15 inches (with the bird sitting on your hand) the subtle shading difference is fairly easy to note.

This little nuthatch's diet in the wild is a mixture of pine cone seeds and bark insects and larva in winter, and insects, primarily small beetles, in the spring and summer. You may succeed in attracting them to your backyard feeder if you provide a steady supply of sunflower seeds and suet.

*Left: A Red-breasted Nuthatch, on the right, appears unconcerned with this chickadee's protest.*

It is impossible, for me at least, to clearly describe the voice of a Red-breasted Nuthatch. In contrast to the loud yank or ank of its white-breasted cousin, the Red-breasted Nuthatch emits a thin, softer, higher enk. Some will say their voice has a nasal hint to it, but I cannot hear that. *Peterson's Eastern Birds* field guide suggests the sound resembles that of a "tiny tin horn." Poetic perhaps, but a bit of a stretch to my ear.

From information gathered at Audubon banding stations, we learn that Red-breasted Nuthatches, if they can outwit their predator enemies, can live to seven or eight years and occasionally a year or two longer.

The first time I landed a Red-breasted Nuthatch was more accidental than planned. That blustery mid-January day is still vivid in my mind. It was 1988 and I was visiting the Ipswich Wildlife Sanctuary 30 miles north of Boston. The temperature was hovering around 20 degrees. Conditions for hand-feeding were ideal, with a foot of snow blanketing the ground. The only other human visitors in the sanctuary were occasional snow skiers. I had not visited this woodland area over the New Year's weekend and, with the two-week gap, the many chickadees who recognize me seemed most eager to avail themselves of a free meal. Once or twice each winter, when the conditions are just right, I will witness what I can only describe as a feeding frenzy with the chickadees. This day was certainly such an occasion. The Black-caps were everywhere; on trees and shrubs all around me, darting back and forth without pause for more than a half hour. As usual, they would eat five or six seeds, then begin hiding seeds for future reference.

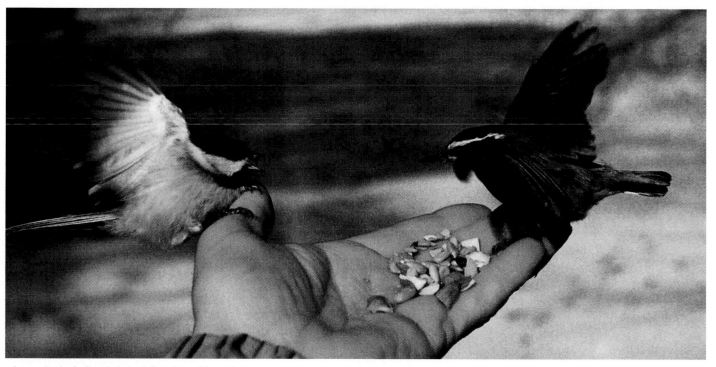

*Above: A battle of wills! Chickadee (left) and a Red-breasted Nuthatch arrived on the hand at exactly the same moment. The more aggressive nuthatch prevailed and the black cap flew off.*

Eventually I noticed a solitary Red-breasted Nuthatch on a limb perhaps ten feet away. He was motionless, but intently studying the beehive of activity going on around me. He remained stock still for what must have been 15 minutes — just observing. I wondered if I could encourage him to take a seed, all the while thinking this was probably unlikely. I had heard of a Red-breasted Nuthatch coming occasionally to a human hand, but had never seen it happen. I assumed they were simply programmed by nature (unlike chickadees) not to invest that much trust in a human being.

Finally I began moving toward him, hand extended, ever so slowly. Inching my way along, I managed to come to within four feet of him before he flew away. I backed up to my starting point and continued feeding the chickadees. In a minute or two, the Red-breast returned to its original perch and continued to survey the scene. I could sense that he wanted to come for a handout, but still he held back. Imperceptibly, I began moving toward him again, stopping about half way. Meanwhile, the Black-caps were zipping in and out, having a great time. Then it happened. With no warning, the nuthatch shot to my hand, snatched a seed and, without really landing, darted back to his perch. I remember thinking, "I've got you!" Sure enough, emboldened by his success, he was back and forth several times before I ran out of seeds. My conclusion is that the feeding frenzy atmosphere surrounding me on that day was the reason this single Red-breasted Nuthatch finally broke through his instinctive caution.

When I returned to that spot the following weekend, there were no Red-breasted Nuthatches in evidence, and I wondered if that individual I had fed was just a solitary fellow moving through the area. I was disappointed not seeing him, since I hoped, having had success with him, he would be a "regular" from then on.

The weekend after that I went back to the same area near the Rockery, still in hopes of seeing this individual. The chickadees were doing their usual thing, the weather was sunny and thirtyish, and I was not in a hurry. Eventually I spotted two Red-breasted Nuthatches on a limb nearby. I kept an eye on them, wondering if either of them was my friend of two weeks ago. Sure enough, one of them flew over and took up a perch several feet over my head. He watched the Black-caps coming and going for several minutes, then dropped down to my index finger. Off he went to enjoy his tidbit of walnut meat. The second nuthatch did not venture closer. My new friend came to my hand several times that morning, and I sensed he would be a regular hand visitor from then on. I scattered a handful of seed on the ground as I left the area, to be sure his mate would have a meal.

Off and on for the rest of that winter I hand-fed this solitary Red-breasted Nuthatch. I wondered in April if he would be there in the fall.

When I returned in October of 1988, I saw no Red-breasted Nuthatches on my first three visits. On the fourth occasion, I was treated to the presence of three Red-breasts. After watching the chickadees hand-feed for several minutes, one of the three nuthatches approached and landed on a twig just beyond my reach. Although there was no way I could be certain, I sensed that this was my friend from the previous winter. Sure enough, he jumped onto my hand and selected a sunflower seed. Off he went to join his companions, neither of whom seemed the least bit inclined to join in the fun. Until I concluded my visit to that spot, this one nuthatch made several more landings, stashing most of the seeds in chinks of bark for retrieval later on. On subsequent visits that winter, I usually encountered this threesome, but was not successful in further efforts to hand-feed nuthatches two and three.

Red-breasted Nuthatches appear to be much less locked into an area than are their larger counterparts, the White-breasts. In my own backyard and at the several sanctuaries I visit, I can count on seeing what are almost surely the same White-breasted Nuthatches in the same area every time. Not so with the Red-breasted Nuthatches.

*Above: A classic "field mark" of the Red-breasted Nuthatch is the bold white stripe just above its eyes.*

At the beginning of this chapter I noted there were two ways I have used to bring Red-breasted Nuthatches to my hand. One, as described above, was learning by observation. When this much more instinctively cautious nuthatch (who was now a frequent hand-feeder) decided that I was not a threat after observing dozens of chickadees hand-feeding, he eventually landed. Once a wild bird lands on a human hand, he or she will almost always return to hand-feed again.

The second way I have approached Red-breasted Nuthatches was through setting the table. In the last four winters, I have encouraged ten or a dozen Red-breasts to come to my hand by this method. Briefly, this involves scattering a handful of seeds on a stump or on the ground where this bird has been seen. Retreat fifteen feet or so and, in a few minutes, any birds in that area will soon come to the seed. Take care to remain very still, and, in a short time it will be as if you have disappeared. Once the Red-breasted Nuthatches have begun feeding, you can slowly close the gap between yourself and the food. This process, as described in the earlier "How-to" chapter, does not happen quickly. Several visits to the same spot will be necessary and your patience will be tested. The birds will eventually accept your non-threatening presence and you may, with a little luck, have a Red-breasted Nuthatch perched on your hand.

It is fun to name individual birds who hand-feed, as I did with several chickadees. This is not so easy with nuthatches since they are quite scarce compared with Black-caps, and the chance of spotting an individual Red- breasted Nuthatch who is not an exact clone of his brothers or sisters is very small.

*Below: A Red-breasted Nuthatch selects from a handful of choice seed and nut meats.*

# Chapter Eight—Other Species

I have been asked how many different species of birds I expect to bring to my hand during my lifetime. My answer is simple: I really do not know, and I am reluctant to venture a guess.

It has never been my intention to acquire a long list of birds which I have succeeded in hand-feeding. I must admit that simple human curiosity prompts me to continue experimenting with wild birds other than the several species discussed in the previous chapters. There is an element of challenge involved, and I suspect that, with extreme patience and an extraordinary investment in time, a few individuals of almost every family of birds can be brought to hand.

Time, of course, is a paramount consideration. For people who are working a 40-hour week, raising a family, and participating in school and civic affairs, finding enough discretionary time to encourage a bird to come to the hand may not be possible. Nevertheless, there is a small percentage of the general population who, due to circumstances of retirement or unusual interest in this activity, will find the time to experiment with hand-feeding wild birds.

I have come very close to having Blue Jays, Cardinals, Downy Woodpeckers and White-throated Sparrows perch on my hand. On a vacation visit to Florida, much to my surprise, I hand-fed Boat-tailed Grackles and Scrub Jays within an hour of encountering them. What follows are summaries of my experiences with these and other species of wild birds over the last twelve years.

## Blue Jays

Those of us who feed the birds in our yards are aware that Blue Jays fly away immediately at the first sign of human activity. I would put jays well down on a list of birds which might be encouraged to hand-feed.

Blue Jays do not rank high in popularity polls with most "birders." Jays are brash and aggressive and people find these traits somehow offensive. Mine is probably a minority opinion; I confess that I love Blue Jays. Their forthright ways appeal to me; they appear to love life and see no need to apologize for that.

Study a jay through your binoculars. We take Blue Jays for granted because they are quite common. If they were an endangered species I think we would appreciate them for the truly beautiful bird they are.

Blue jays love cheese crackers! We have a ten-inch-wide deck railing in back of our house which is perfect for setting out tidbits of food for the birds. During the months from November through March we usually start the day by scattering a little sunflower seed, bread crusts, and cheese crackers along this railing. The resident flock of Blue Jays, numbering eight birds this past winter, will quite literally call me out of bed at 7:00 A.M. if their morning treats are not in evidence. In a mix of feed, the jays

*Left Page: The author's wife, Barbara hand-feeds a flock of seagulls on the ferry to Nantucket.*
*Below: A Blue Jay on the porch railing prepares to depart with a cheese cracker.*

invariably head straight for the cheese crackers. Here is how I coaxed one jay to take a cracker from my hand.

I had long wondered if it was possible to bring a Blue Jay onto my hand and eventually photograph the event. Beginning last December, we made a point of faithfully placing 15 or 20 "Cheese Its" on the railing at about 6:45 A.M. Within minutes, the jays were there. They would break the crackers into bite-sized pieces with their beaks, eat a cracker or two then carry whole crackers away for future indulgence. Soon the jays assumed that this

*Left: A brave Blue Jay snatches a cheese cracker while the rest of his group observes from a nearby tree. This photo was taken at a distance of 6 feet.*

ritual would occur every morning. I could usually see them perched in the maple tree nearby, as I walked out to the railing early in the morning. Within three or four minutes, the last of the cheese crackers were gone. Soon the bolder jays were on the railing before I had stepped back into the house. At this point, I decided to try to hand-feed at least one Blue Jay before spring arrived. The way to accomplish this was to gradually reduce the distance between myself and the jays after putting out the crackers.

Over the next several weeks this feeding ritual continued. In the beginning I would walk the eight feet back to (but not through) the sliding door, then stop and remain perfectly still. With little hesitation the jays came to the railing to take the cheese crackers. Soon the jays seemed oblivious to my presence, even though I was standing only eight feet away in full view. Ever so slowly, over four or five weeks, I closed the gap to three feet. At this point, even though I stood stock still, the Blue Jays would land six or eight feet down the railing, and would wait for me to back off a step or two. When I moved back to a distance of four or five feet, they would hop over and take their crackers. I seemed to have reached a barrier which the jays were reluctant to cross.

After two weeks of backing off a foot or two, I decided to hold my ground. For a full ten minutes I stood there without moving, just a yardstick from the railing. Five jays took up a position six feet away, expecting me to back off as I had done in the past. I stayed put. Finally my patience was rewarded. The largest jay, appearing to be the dominant bird in the group, hopped across the rail, snatched a cracker and darted off to the maple tree. The other jays did not move. The lead jay came back twice, directly to the rail in front of me, and flew off to consume his crackers. Than he flew away, followed by his mates. I put several crackers on the railing and went inside, feeling good that another small barrier had been crossed.

In the three or four weeks that followed, this one jay continued to take crackers from the rail while just three feet from me, as long as I remained motionless. His companions would always wait until I took two steps backward before they would hop over to the crackers.

One morning early in March, I took a position a foot from the railing and placed my hand, holding three cheese crackers, on the rail. As usual, the Blue Jays flew to the railing six to eight feet away. After a minute or two, the lead jay hopped to my hand, reached over, took a cracker, and was gone. Another little barrier broken through. Although the rest of the flock watched this action intently, none of the others came closer to my hand than five feet. The dominant bird was now willing to walk up to my hand with no further hesitation, as long as there was no motion on my part. My efforts to photograph this from the railing have been fruitless. As soon as there is the least motion, the bird is gone.

I hope to have this individual Blue Jay sitting on my hand next winter. Whether or not I will be able to photograph this event remains to be seen.

## Downy Woodpecker

For many winters, we have hung a couple of suet feeders in trees behind our house. These feeders help a variety of birds to get through our harsh New England winters. Regulars are Hairy and Downy Woodpeckers, nuthatches, chickadees, titmice, jays, an occasional Mockingbird and, of course, the ever present Starlings. We start with the suet in November, and keep a steady supply available through mid-April.

As I replenished the suet holders, I noticed that if there happened to be a Downy Woodpecker on the cage, I could approach the bird, moving slowly, to within four or five feet before it flew off. Hairy Woodpeckers, a similar but larger bird, would not permit me to come closer than 25 to 30 feet before flying away. Once the Downys have become accustomed to feeding regularly at a safe suet station, they tend to become quite tolerant of humans nearby.

Last winter I decided to spend some time in an effort to bring a Downy Woodpecker to my hand. I had observed that a pair of these little woodpeckers were showing up almost every evening before dusk. The male, identified as such by a bright red dot on the back of his head, would go to the suet first. A minute or two later, his mate would follow. They would dine for several minutes and than fly off until the next morning. Two or three evenings a week I began to walk very slowly toward the feeders while these birds were feeding. The more slowly I moved, the closer I was able to approach before they flew away. Before a month went by, I was standing just three feet away from the suet cage before the male departed. The female flew off when I came to within six feet.

Left: This shy Downy Woodpecker was photographed at a distance of 4 feet at the backyard suet feeder. The red coloring on its head identifies it as a male.

Eventually I changed the location of the suet cage. I hung it so that it was nearly touching the main trunk of the maple tree. In the evening I would walk, again barely moving, to the suet cage while the woodpeckers were feeding. After two weeks, (three evenings a week for a half hour at a time) the pair of downys accepted my silent approach without any sign of apprehension. I felt it was time to try hand-feeding.

Next, I removed the suet basket entirely. That evening, about the time the pair arrived, I went to the maple tree with bits of suet in my hand. Sure enough, the Downys arrived right on schedule and landed on a branch several feet over my head. I rested my hand against the trunk of the tree where the suet holder had been and waited. Several minutes went by, with the two birds flitting to and fro above my head, but not coming closer. After ten minutes I decided to replace the basket, and retreated to the house. Before I reached the back door, both downys were on the suet.

I repeated this process for several evenings with little apparent progress. I was concerned that this pair of woodpeckers was becoming acclimated to the probability that, after 10 or 15 minutes, this human would replace the feeder and retreat to the house.

The next evening I decided to stay at the tree for an hour, to see what would happen. Predictably, the pair of Downy Woodpeckers landed five feet over my head and proceeded to wait me out. Twenty minutes went by and it appeared to me that I might just be wasting my time. Then I noticed that the male was becoming increasingly agitated. He was flitting around now, and was clearly scolding me. I held my ground, remaining absolutely still. Finally my stubbornness was rewarded. Mr. Downy flew down to the trunk and landed a foot above my hand. He studied me intently for a minute, then flew back to his mate. Back he came to the same spot, head down, waiting. After what seemed like several minutes, he walked down to my hand, reached over my index finger, picked out a piece of suet and flew directly to his mate. He poked the suet into Mrs. Downy's mouth and returned to me. Again he walked to my hand and took more suet. This time he swallowed a piece, then selected another bit and flew back to feed his mate. I must confess to a feeling of exhilaration as I watched this scene play out.

Although this male woodpecker continued on successive evenings to take suet from my hand while he clung to the tree trunk, he would not jump to my hand when I stood back.

With the arrival of spring and a busier schedule, I abandoned this little project, to be continued in November. It will be interesting to see if this same pair returns to our suet feeders next November. With a little more time I am confident that eventually I will photograph the male standing on my hand.

*Below: A vibrant-colored male Cardinal makes for a marvelous subject. In this case, Carleton (described on the next page) became one of the author's most cherished photographs. Photo was taken at a distance of 5 feet.*

## Cardinal

In an eastern Massachusetts wildlife sanctuary I became quite friendly with a resident male Cardinal.

I met this fellow several winters ago while sitting on a stone wall near a quiet pond. At the other end of this low 15-foot wall a mix of birds were availing themselves of seeds, nut meats, and bread crumbs in my efforts toward hand-feeding a pair of White-breasted Nuthatches. Without warning, a male Cardinal dropped down from a nearby shrub and began cracking open sunflower seeds. I had never been this close to a Cardinal, and I recall how impressive his brilliant scarlet feathers were in the full sunlight. As long as I remained motionless, he, in the company of chickadees, titmice, nuthatches, a Downy Woodpecker and several White-throated Sparrows, continued to feed. Off in the brush and up the path, I detected the female Cardinal, seemingly uninterested in joining the picnic.

After five minutes, fully satisfied, the Cardinal flew off.

In succeeding weekend visits to this spot, I moved closer along the wall toward the feeding area. Mr. Cardinal was almost always in attendance, and I could usually detect his mate somewhere close-by. As long as I imitated a statue, "Carleton," as I had named this bird, accepted my presence. At my slightest motion, accidental or otherwise, he would take wing. The point at which I could go no closer to him was about six feet. As you can see from the photo, Carleton Cardinal is a strikingly handsome fellow.

Cardinals are quite territorial. They rarely stray more than a hundred yards from their nesting area. Males defend their turf against other male Cardinals and the same individuals can almost always be seen or heard when you enter their neighborhood.

So it was, and still is, with Carleton. I am sure he recognizes me, and I can scatter seed on the stone wall six or seven feet away, sit down and await his company. Occasionally, he will crack open a seed, fly up to his mate, feed her, and return. For whatever reason, Mrs. Cardinal will not come to the wall.

I have not seriously tried to hand-feed this bird, partly because of the time involved, and partly because we are mutually happy to know each other at a distance of six feet. This past winter was the fourth year of our informal association, and maybe next winter I will attempt to hand-feed him.

## White-Throated Sparrows

White-throated Sparrows are unusually handsome little birds. The male, especially, is strikingly marked, with black and white stripes along the head and a bright yellow spot above and in front of its eyes. Just beneath its bill is a sharply defined white throat patch. If you have an opportunity, study this bird with the aid of your binoculars.

White-throated Sparrows appear not to be affected by the general decline of bird populations here in the northeast. White-throats are quite

*Below: A colorful White-throated Sparrow inspects the food scattered along a brick wall to attract titmice and nuthatches. White-throats, with time, can probably be encouraged to hand-feed. This photo was taken at a distance of 6 feet.*

common in our woodlands and sanctuaries and I never tire of admiring them. Curiously, these birds are rarely seen above the ground. Their entire existence seems to involve a constant scrabbling around in the underbrush, turning over leaves in search of seeds and insects.

Although I have never made an effort to hand-feed a White-throat, they are probably likely candidates for this activity. They will tolerate human presence quite readily, and I have often sat on a log or stone fence within five feet of these sparrows to watch them feed. Perhaps next winter I shall try my luck with White-throated Sparrows.

## Scrub Jay

*Right: A Scrub Jay flys off after deciding this bit of cracker was not to its liking. Scrub Jays are making a comeback in Florida after many years of declining numbers.*

Further afield, I happened to spot three Scrub Jays in a tree near Sarasota, Florida last winter. From several sources I had heard and read that this cousin of our northern Blue Jay is quite amenable to taking food from human hands.

The primary range of Scrub Jays exists from the far west of Washington, Wyoming, and Nebraska, through Texas and into Mexico. Their secondary, and much smaller range, is the scrub oak areas of central and southern Florida.

On a whim we stopped to try our luck at hand-feeding. To my great surprise, two of the three Scrub Jays were coming to my hand in less than ten minutes. One of these birds was banded, attesting to prior human contact. These two birds were back and forth to my hand several times for bread scraps, and seemed not the least bit putoff by the presence and the click of my camera. In a note received from Roger Tory Peterson a year ago, Mr. Peterson attests to the relative ease of hand-feeding Scrub Jays during his visits to Florida in years past.

## Boat-tailed Grackle

On this same vacation trip to Florida, I had an opportunity to attempt to hand-feed several Boat-tailed Grackles at a public beach near Venice. A friend had mentioned to me years ago that this large cousin of our common Purple Grackle will occasionally hand-feed with very little introductory efforts.

The chocolate brown female Boat-tailed Grackle is noticeably smaller than the purple-black male. For reasons unknown to me, the males are skittish of close human contact, while the females seem quite ready to accept a hand-out. With pre-focused camera and a small supply of bread crusts in hand, I sat down on a shady section of beach and scattered several bits of bread close by. Immediately, several females walked to within 18 inches of my feet and began to feed. Holding my camera in my right hand, I extended my left hand, with bread, to ground level. After momentary hesitation, a female grackle walked up to my hand, casually picked out a bit of bread, and walked away. I was so surprised I forgot to attempt a photograph. Not to worry; a minute later she was back for more, not the least bit apprehensive, and the accompanying photo resulted.

Perhaps this flock of grackles had become used to taking food from humans at that particular beach area.

## Miscellaneous

The number of other species of birds which have taken food directly from a human hand will never be known. This number is probably much larger than we would guess.

In his book ***Hand-Taming Wild Birds at the Feeder***, Maine resident Alfred G. Martin tells of hand-feeding several species of birds not often seen today in Massachusetts, including Redpolls, Pine Siskins, Evening Grosbeaks, Canada Jays, Pine Grosbeaks, and an occasional Yellow-bellied Sapsucker. Martin tried for years to hand-feed White-breasted Nuthatches, without success.

I have read that Ruby-throated Hummingbirds will hand-feed, but I see them so rarely that it would be nearly impossible to experiment with one.

Many sea birds can become quite habituated to close human contact. Examples are seagulls, and in the south, pelicans. At Florida beaches, we have had Ruddy Turnstones, Sanderlings, and Sandpipers come close, with little hesitation, for scraps of bread. My guess is that, with time and patience, individuals of these and other shore bird species can be coaxed onto a human hand.

Below: While hand-feeding seagulls, Barbara Wiberg's only concern was the possibility of having her fingers accidentally pecked.

# Chapter Nine—Photographing Birds on the Hand

Several years ago, I saw in a Boston newspaper a photograph of a chickadee standing on a woman's hand. The caption accompanying the picture noted that the lady's husband took the photo in their backyard. I was quite taken with that picture. I had been hand-feeding Black-caps for many years and never gave serious thought to photographing a bird on my hand. What were the chances, after all, of taking a quality picture of a bird on the left hand while holding a camera in the right hand? I set out to see if it could be done.

I lay no claim to being a great photographer. Like most dads, I took many 35 mm pictures of my three children through the years. During the 1970s I volunteered to take, on a part-time basis, sports photographs for the local weekly newspaper. My picture-taking skills, such as they may be, are not on a professional-quality level.

Through much trial and error over the last three years, I have arrived at a point where I am no longer embarrassed to share photos I have taken of birds on my hand. The first several rolls of pictures were so poor (with one or two exceptions) that I set them aside and nearly abandoned the project. But, being a stubborn Swede, I pressed on.

There are two major factors working against the would-be photographer in such an attempt. The first is that the simple act of raising the camera to the eye will spook the bird because there is motion involved. Secondly, a bird standing on the hand is there for only a second or two. This leaves very little time to adjust the camera for exposure and focus before snapping the shutter. At first it appeared to me that these obstacles would be insurmountable.

In order to eventually take a respectable picture of a bird standing on one's hand, it is first necessary to arrive at very friendly and trusting terms

*Left Page: Holding a pre-focused Pentax K-1000 camera in his right hand, Hugh Wiberg "shoots" a Scrub Jay near Sarasota, Florida. Original photo by Barbara Wiberg.*

*Right: More often than not, a novice photographer of hand-fed birds will achieve this result. Here, the shutter was depressed one second too late to catch the nuthatch on the hand.*

with the subject bird. Black-capped Chickadees are the ideal species to photograph in the beginning, since, as we have learned, they are by far the easiest bird to hand-feed. Before attempting the very first photo session, it is necessary that you have conditioned (or have found) one or more chickadees who will come to your hand regularly and with confidence. Let's assume you have arrived at that point and it is time to experiment with your camera.

As to equipment, any reasonably good quality 35 mm camera will do. I happen to have a Pentax K 1000 with both automatic and manual capabilities. The photos in this book, with a few exceptions, were taken with this camera. I have tried all of the available color films and eventually settled on Kodak Gold 200.

*Left: While vacationing in Florida, the author tried his luck hand-feeding and photographing Scrub Jays near Sarasota. A resident on bended knee soon landed a Scrub Jay on his hat!*
*Above: The "click" of a shutter is enough to startle a model titmouse. In this case, a slow shutter speed was not fast enough to capture and freeze the wing motion.*
*Below: Depth of field decisions are critical when photographing at such a short distance. Here the bird is out of focus while the hand is clearly pictured.*

After many failed attempts to take a respectable picture of a bird on my hand, I finally resolved the problem of motion frightening away the birds. Step one does not involve the camera at all. The camera is hanging from

*Above: This photo was taken at the relatively slow shutter speed of 1/250 second. Had it been snapped at 1/1000 second, the chickadee's wing motion would have been eliminated.*
*Below: A straight-on shot of a Tufted Titmouse does nothing in describing the beauty of this bird. In most cases, profile shots make for better wild bird photographs.*

the shoulder, ready for use in a while. Having encountered my subjects, I offer food in the left hand. Soon the chickadees are racing back and forth to my hand, reinforcing and strengthening the rapport we have enjoyed from many previous encounters. After 15 or 20 landings (usually ten minutes or so), it is time to bring the camera into play.

Risking puzzled looks from passersby, I raise the cocked and pre-focused camera to my eye, while continuing to extend the left hand with food. No further motion occurs now and, within a minute of two the birds who have been hand-feeding begin to return. I am looking through the view finder at my hand, waiting for a chickadee. The bird lands and it is decision time. If the Black-cap lands directly facing the camera, it is best to pass up the opportunity. Birds photograph to best advantage when they land with body in full view. Typically, a Black-capped Chickadee will alight, select a bit of food, hesitate a split second, and then disappear, all in about two seconds. The photographer, in the beginning, will click the shutter immediately after the bird has landed, knowing the available time span is very short.

Thus, we have resolved the motion problem by standing ready, camera positioned, waiting for a landing.

As to the second problem (no time to make exposure and lighting adjustments), we get over this hurdle by making our camera adjustments

Shutter speed of 1/500th second could not "stop" the motion in this photo. Best results are obtained when camera is set at 1/1000th second.

before the landing. In average sunny conditions, I will set my camera at 1/1000 second and F 8 to 11. In order to stop any wing motion, it is necessary to set the speed dial at 1/1000 second. A setting slower than this setting and your camera will not freeze wing motion. Sharp focus is achieved by pre-focusing the camera, sighting on the tips of the fingers of your left hand. We are fighting a "depth of field" problem here, shooting at this very close-up setting. (Depth of field refers to the narrow band — usually an inch or a little less — in which our subject will be in sharp focus at a distance of 18 to 24 inches.)

Once these initial problems are understood and reconciled, photographing birds on your hand becomes a matter of trial and error, with, at first, the emphasis on error. After the first winter of experimenting, during which I may have exposed a dozen, 24-frame films. I looked for two or three good quality photos from each film. After two additional winters of practice, I now expect five or six decent pictures from each roll.

Above: "Depth of field" is critical when photographing birds at 16 inches. Note that the seed is in focus, while this titmouse's head, only an inch or so further away, is slightly out of focus. Below: A faster shutter speed would have "frozen" movement in this group photo of black caps and nuthatch.

# Chapter 10—Is Hand-Feeding Intrusive?

It may be useful to begin this chapter by defining the word "intrusive."

*Above: A White-breasted Nuthatch, learning to hand-feed, selects a piece of nut meat from the author's hand.*

Intrusive, in the context of hand-feeding wild birds, means engaging in an activity which, due to behavior modification, might put the birds' well-being in jeopardy. It has been suggested to me that encouraging wild birds to hand-feed will dispose the birds to also trust those who could harm them. Further, it is proposed, hand-feeding wild birds will make the birds dependent on those who regularly hand-feed them. These issues must be addressed.

As to whether hand-feeding wild birds brings any dangers to the birds so conditioned, 15 years of experience leads me to believe that this does not happen. I have yet to see (or hear of) a single instance in which a bird that has learned to hand-feed has been threatened or harmed by a human. People who are visiting wildlife sanctuaries, state parks, and other woodland areas are not people who would go out of their way to bring harm to the resident wildlife. In frequent visits to woodlands and sanctuaries, the people I meet and chat with are invariably respecters of wildlife, including those few birds which have learned to hand-feed.

All of this notwithstanding, I do not profess to be the final authority on the matter of possible intrusiveness as it may relate to hand-feeding birds. Recently I contacted ten professionals in the field of birding, either authors of bird books or people otherwise engaged in some aspect of ornithology. I was favored with replies from eight of the ten and the respondents were unanimous: hand-feeding wild birds is not intrusive. Typical of the replies were:

"I have spent time at my feeder trying to get chickadees to land (on my hand). I can't remember if any did, but I never thought of it as intrusive." **Michael Corral**, author of several bird books, including *The World of Birds*, published by Globe Pequot Press.

"I would not consider hand-feeding wild birds any more intrusive than setting up a bird feeder in the back yard." **Donald Hyde**, president of the Hyde Bird Feeder Company, Waltham, Massachusetts.

"After my many years in the field of ornithology, I would agree with your contention that hand-feeding wild birds is not intrusive." **John V. Dennis**, author of more than a dozen bird books, including *A Complete Guide To Bird Feeding*, published by Alfred Knopf.

I was also favored with a response from a man who most birders consider to be the foremost authority on birds in the world, **Dr. Roger Tory Peterson**. (My question was, as with the other respondents: "Would you consider hand-feeding wild birds to be harmfully intrusive?") With Dr. Peterson's kind permission, I quote from one of his letters: "You posed the question, does feeding birds from the hand impose any intrusive dangers? Absolutely not, so far as I have observed. I have fed many a chickadee from my hands, as well as nuthatches, titmice, and several other birds. I have never seen anyone take unethical advantage of the situation." Dr. Roger Tory Peterson - April, 1992.

The University of Wisconsin's Department of Wildlife Ecology recently concluded a carefully controlled experiment on whether birds feeding at our backyard feeders will lose their instinctive abilities to survive. The results of this study were reported in the spring 1992 issue of the Journal of Field Ornithology. One of the questions the researchers addressed was, "Will wild birds lose some or all of their natural abilities to survive our harsh winters as a result of the generosity of the millions of Americans [and Canadians, among others] who tend bird feeders?" To answer this question, two groups of chickadees were monitored over several years. The first group had no possible association with bird feeders, while the second group was fed regularly for three years before being cut off from their bird feeder handouts. The two groups were then studied during the following several winters, and there was no measurable difference in the rate of survival between the groups. (My thanks to **Dr. Stanley Temple** of the University of Wisconsin's Department of Wildlife Ecology for his permission to quote from our March 1993 telephone conservation.)

This study was of great interest to me, since I have long believed, but have not been able to prove, that the birds I hand-fed from October to March suffered no ill effects when April came and I, along with other hand-feeders, had left. This belief stems from observing several birds I came to recognize due to their physical differences, who returned to me after a six-month separation, seeming fit and healthy. Peg Leg, a chickadee discussed in Chapter 4, was a classic example.

The University of Wisconsin's controlled experiment appears to validate my contention that birds who hand-feed over many months are not placed in jeopardy when their human benefactors stop hand-feeding in March or April.

## A Closing Thought

I think of myself as being a concerned naturalist. Pollution and environmental degradation in whatever form appall me, since their negative effects on wildlife are well documented. The erosion of the rain forests in Central and South America is a true modern day tragedy, resulting in the serious decline in the numbers of birds which winter in that area and summer in the United States and Canada.

All true lovers of nature have an obligation to their children and grandchildren to become actively involved in matters relating to the destruction of wildlife habitats world-wide.

*Below: No sooner does one chickadee fly off, than another arrives.*

Above: A Red-breasted Nuthatch prepares to launch after selecting a bit of nut meat from the hand of the author.
Below: A Tufted Titmouse on the left waits his turn as the chickadee on the left moves-in for a nut meat.

## Other Books Published By
# Annedawn Publishing

Annedawn Publishing **is proud to make this and other books available. For information on how you can receive a copy of any of the following books, write to** Annedawn Publishing, Box 247-Bird, Norton, MA 02766 or ask your bookstore to order a copy for you from their book supplier.

## Hand-Feeding Wild Birds

## How-to-Grow World Class Giant Pumpkins

THE GROWING
AND
MARKETING
OF FALL MUMS

How You Can Turn Your Backyard Into. . .
A Money-Making Growing Machine!
Don Langevin

## The Growing and Marketing of Fall Mums